Everlasting FATHER

OTHER TITLES IN THIS CHRISTMAS SERIES

And He Shall Be Called...Wonderful Counselor
by Larry Libby and Steve Halliday

And He Shall Be Called...Mighty God
by Steve Halliday

AND HE SHALL BE CALLED...

Everlasting FATHER

REDISCOVERING THE FIRST CHRISTMAS GIFT

STEVE HALLIDAY &
ED YOUNG

WATERBROOK
PRESS

EVERLASTING FATHER
PUBLISHED BY WATERBROOK PRESS
2375 Telstar Drive, Suite 160
Colorado Springs, Colorado 80920
A division of Random House, Inc.

ISBN 1-57856-317-8

Library of Congress Cataloging-in-Publication Data
Halliday, Steve, 1957–
    And He shall be called Everlasting Father : rediscovering the first
Christmas gift / Steve Halliday and Ed Young.—1st ed.
        p. cm.
Includes bibliographical references.
    ISBN 1-57856-317-8
    1. Christmas—Meditations.   I. Young, H. Edwin, 1936–   II. Title.
    BV45 .H325 2002
    242'.335—dc21

                                                    2002006905

Printed in the United States of America
2002—First Edition

10 9 8 7 6 5 4 3 2 1

CONTENTS

Introduction: Watch Him Sparkle 1

1. The Son Who Was Always a Father 7

2. See One, See the Other 21

3. *The Hedge* 35

4. The Open Vault 47

5. Tidings of Comfort and Joy 59

6. *Just As He Said* 73

7. Measuring the Immeasurable 85

8. With Us All the Time 99

9. *The Journal* 113

10. A Cure for Troubled Hearts 125

11. A Prodigal Christmas 139

12. *Nativity Lemons* 151

13. There's No Place Like Home 161

14. *The Composition* 171

Notes 183

Let us follow the Magi. Let us separate ourselves from our barbarian customs and leave them far behind, for only in that way may we see Christ. Had they not traveled far from their own country, they too would have missed seeing Him. While they remained in Persia, they saw only the star; but after they departed, they beheld the Sun of Righteousness. So let us also rise up. Though troubles hound us, let us run to the house of the young Child. Though kings and nations and tyrants interrupt our journey, let us ever pursue this desire. For so shall we thoroughly repel all the dangers that beset us.

—Saint John Chrysostom[1]

WATCH HIM SPARKLE

*F*ocus is everything. Lose it, and eventually you end up where you never wanted to be. That's especially true at Christmas. With all of the season's bright lights, pretty paper, cute programs, and a thousand other fun activities all clamoring for our attention, it's altogether too easy to lose our focus on the beating heart of Christmas, Jesus Christ Himself. We simply can't allow that to happen. We can't afford to lose sight of Jesus, for only with Him at the center will our holiday celebrations bring us the joy and satisfaction that we crave.

But if that's true, then shouldn't we be asking ourselves a question? Namely, *How can we dedicate ourselves this season to regaining a strong focus on Jesus?*

What *is* the best way to keep our focus on Christ? Should we cut out all the traditional Christmas accouterment—gift giving, decorated trees, presents, cards, parties, lights, goodies—and spend all our time poring over the Nativity story as recorded in the Gospels? Should we spurn all things cultural and use every spare moment for quiet contemplation of the Lord's incarnation?

In other words, if Jesus is the Reason for the Season, then does Rudolph give a mule ride of a yuletide?

We don't think so.

We best honor a diamond not by trying to hide lesser stones, but by holding the diamond up to the light and allowing the fiery rays of the sun to reveal the jewel's sparkling perfection. The best way to maintain our focus on the diamond is to closely observe its glowing radiance and to marvel at its faultless clarity, color, and cut, not to look down at the dirt while trampling rhinestones.

We think the same is true of keeping our focus on Jesus during the Christmas season. The best way to keep Him at the center of our celebrations is to spend some unhurried time marveling at His perfection and majesty, not by trying to avoid the distractions of a seriously overcommercialized holiday. We best honor Jesus not by consciously looking away from other things, but by eagerly fixing our gaze upon *Him*.

In this book, the third in a series, we want to focus on our Lord as He is revealed by the prophet Isaiah in a famous Christmas-flavored passage:

For to us a child is born,
> to us a son is given,
> and the government will be on his shoulders.
And he will be called…
> *Everlasting Father.* (9:6)

The two previous volumes in this Christmas series focused on Jesus Christ as our Wonderful Counselor and as our Mighty God. In this work, we would like to turn our attention to the Son of God as He reveals Himself to be our Everlasting Father.

Yet even before we dot another *i,* we run into a bit of a problem.

The fact is, most of us aren't used to thinking of Jesus Christ as our Father. Everlasting? Sure—but *Father?* It sounds so confusing. As Christians, we believe in God the Father, God the Son, and God the Holy Spirit. Why complicate matters (already deeply mysterious) by trying to ponder God the Son as *Father?*

Even the Christmas carols we sing each year, the cherished songs that bring such tradition and richness to the season of Noel, shy away from exploring the idea of Jesus as our Everlasting Father. They speak clearly and often about the other titles Isaiah gives to the Christ but seem to avoid this one.

The old carols joyfully praise Isaiah's "Wonderful Counselor" when they laud Jesus as the "infant of wonder" and speak of Him as "wisdom from on high."

They revel in "Mighty God" by lifting up the "God of Might" and by proclaiming Jesus the "Incarnate Deity."

They celebrate the "Prince of Peace" by ascribing that exact title to Jesus.

But of Jesus the "Everlasting Father," we hear little. True, the old carols declare Jesus to be "Alpha and Omega" and call Him "Everlasting Lord"—but never do they whisper a word about His prophetic role as Father. The closest we seem to get is the marvelous title, "Word *of* the Father." Close, but not quite there.

Now, we love the old carols and wouldn't dream of boycotting them on account of this single omission; nevertheless, we consider the oversight regrettable. Isaiah meant to convey something important by bestowing the lofty title of Everlasting Father upon the Messiah, and all of us will be the poorer if we neglect to consider this beautiful facet of Jesus' sparkling character.

In what sense does Isaiah want us to think of Jesus as our Everlasting Father? Certainly, our Lord is eternal; there never was a time when He was not. But how is He our Father?

Scripture declares that Jesus Christ is the Author of Life, the Author of Our Salvation, and the Author of Our Faith

(Acts 3:15; Hebrews 2:10; Hebrews 12:2). In that sense, then, He is our Father because He gives us physical life, He gives us spiritual birth, and He guides and directs our faith. While God the Son remains forever distinct from God the Father, we ought to burst with joy that Jesus Christ treats us as His beloved sons and daughters, just as a loving father would treat his own dear children. Like a father, Jesus

- protects us,
- gives to us,
- encourages us,
- keeps His promises to us,
- loves us,
- reassures us,
- calms us,
- comforts us,
- forgives us,
- sets an example for us,
- prepares a home for us, and
- amazes us.

Our Lord does all this and more.

We invite you now to invest some unhurried moments as we ponder together how our Savior, Jesus Christ, is also our Everlasting Father. To maximize your time, we suggest that you set aside a few hours in the weeks before Christmas to prepare your heart for a wonderful celebration of the

Lord's arrival at Bethlehem so long ago. Try to read a chapter a day for two weeks, pausing throughout the day to turn over in your mind the astonishing love and grace of your Everlasting Father.

We've included both fiction and nonfiction to give you several ways to focus on Jesus. The five fiction chapters are indicated by italics in the table of contents and by a decorative border alongside the story. Chapters written primarily by Steve Halliday are noted by his initials *(S.H.)*, while the letters *E.Y.* indicate the work of Dr. Ed Young.

Are you ready to turn your eyes upon Jesus? If so, start gazing upon the flawless, diamondlike character of Christ. Put your focus on Him and, by doing so, prepare to celebrate the best Christmas ever.

ONE

THE SON WHO WAS ALWAYS A FATHER

But you, Bethlehem Ephrathah,
    though you are small among the clans of Judah,
out of you will come for me
    one who will be ruler over Israel,
whose origins are from of old,
    from ancient times.

MICAH 5:2

*T*here's nothing like having little ones around at Christmastime. Our adult hearts grow warm and sudden laughter bursts from our throats when we watch little eyes grow big with wonder at the growing pile of presents beneath the tree. In a very special way, Christmas really is for kids.

And if you're around kids at Christmas—especially kids

who like to tell jokes—you're bound to be asked a number of holiday riddles. The children I know just can't seem to resist riddles like these:

- What do elves learn in school?
- What do snowmen eat for breakfast?
- What kind of candle burns longer, a red candle or a green candle?
- Why was Santa's little helper depressed?

Now, if you think I'm going to give you the answers to these kid-endorsed riddles just like that, then you've got another thing coming.[1] Riddles are supposed to make you *think*. That's half the fun, to see if you can figure out the answer.

For example, I'll bet you don't have much trouble at all coming up with the right answer to yet another Christmas riddle:

- What Christmas carol is the favorite of parents?

This one is so easy, I don't feel bad giving you the answer: "Silent Night," of course.

Riddles can be a lot of fun, but they also can be extremely significant, depending upon the nature of the riddle and who asks it. Would it surprise you to learn that Jesus Christ Himself once asked a riddle of the ruling powers of His day? They found the riddle so tough, they didn't even attempt an answer. Yet if they had applied a little Christmastime logic to the question, they might have come up with the answer—and found eternal life in the bargain.

I *told* you that some riddles can be very important!

BOTH SON AND LORD?

As the time for Jesus' crucifixion drew near, His opponents stepped up their efforts to discredit Him. Matthew says they "laid plans to trap him in his words" (22:15).

Members of three separate groups, Pharisees, Herodians, and Sadducees—individuals who normally attacked each other but who banded together against Jesus—asked the Lord three tough questions designed to land Him in trouble. Each time, He answered the question and, in the process, revealed the wicked intent of those who asked it. So successfully did He answer the questions that Mark reports, "And from then on no one dared ask him any more questions" (12:34).

But then it was Jesus' turn to ask questions. "What do you think about the Christ?" He asked the Pharisees. "Whose son is He?"

"The Son of David," they answered correctly. Any Jewish schoolboy knew the right answer. But Jesus was not finished. Now it was time for His riddle.

"How is it then," Jesus asked, "that David, speaking by the Spirit, calls him 'Lord'?... If then David calls him 'Lord,' how can he be his son?" (Matthew 22:41-45).

Now the Pharisees usually were the ones asking the questions; they did not like it at all when someone turned the tables. And they especially did not like a puzzler such as this one. Their minds slipped into overdrive, but they managed nothing more than to strip a few gears.

The Messiah is the Son of David because He comes from the line of David, they must have thought. *But why would the great King David call his descendant his lord? No father calls his own son his lord! Much less would a patriarch address his distant heir in such a lofty fashion. So why would David, speaking by the Spirit of God, call this descendant his lord? Why? What could it mean? What? WHAT???*

In the end, because they could give Jesus no answer, they kept silent. And Jesus never offered to reveal the answer. So the riddle remained unsolved.

FINDING THE KEY

Today, by piecing together a few crucial Bible passages, we can solve the riddle that so badly stumped the Pharisees. In the process, not only will we discover the remarkable answer

Jesus had in mind, but we will also find a magnificent key capable of unlocking a meaningful Christmas celebration far beyond anything we may have known.

Everyone in Jesus' day knew that the Messiah, the Christ, would come from the family line of David. Centuries before, when this Jewish king announced his plans to build a temple for the Lord, God stepped in and refused to allow it. Instead, the Almighty said *He* would build a "house" for the *king,* a line of descendants that would "endure forever before me; your throne will be established forever" (2 Samuel 7:16). And from then on, the promised Messiah was known as "the Son of David."

In ancient Israelite culture, however, a father never called his son "my lord." Inferiors used the term *lord* (Hebrew, *adonai*) to address their superiors, and a father by definition could not be inferior to his son—let alone inferior to a distant descendant. Hence the extreme difficulty of Jesus' riddle: How could David call his "son" his lord? It didn't make sense.

The Pharisees might have done better with the riddle had they considered the ancient prophets. Had they remembered the words of Isaiah, for example, they might have guessed the truth. For Isaiah had predicted not only that a Branch (that is, the Messiah) would come *from* the stump and root of David's family, but that somehow this amazing

Person would also be called "the *Root* of Jesse." In other words, not only would He *come* from the root of David's line, but He also *originated* it!

The prophet Micah, a contemporary of Isaiah, expanded on Isaiah's tantalizing hints regarding the true identity of the Messiah. "But you, Bethlehem Ephrathah," he wrote, "though you are small among the clans of Judah, out of you will come for me one who will be ruler over Israel, whose origins are from of old, from ancient times" (5:2).

Every Bible student in Israel recognized that this prophecy foretold the birthplace of the Messiah, the Son of David—appropriately enough, in the hometown of David. Since people in ancient times had called Bethlehem "Ephrathah" (Genesis 35:16,19; Ruth 4:11), the prophet included the old name to distinguish David's ancestral home from other towns named Bethlehem, such as the one in Zebulun (Joshua 19:15). We do a similar thing today to distinguish, say, between Boston, Massachusetts, and Boston, Arkansas (or the other Bostons in Georgia, Indiana, Louisiana, Michigan, Missouri, Tennessee, and Texas).

But what could the prophet possibly have meant when he said that this coming Messiah would have "origins…from of old, from ancient times"? That does not sound like an ordinary son, whether David's or anyone else's.

And in fact, Micah had in mind something far more

than an ordinary son. The term *origins* is, more literally, "his goings forth," and refers to the person's activities. The Hebrew term often has military connotations, as when it describes the departure of an army into battle (see 2 Samuel 3:25, KJV). Apparently, Micah meant to describe this Messiah as a person of great might and power.

And what of the terms *of old* and *ancient times?* These Hebrew words always refer to something of great antiquity, sometimes even of eternal extent; context alone determines the expanse of time meant. Intriguingly, at least one of Micah's predecessors had used the term *qedem* ("of old") to refer to God (Deuteronomy 33:27). So Micah clearly understood this Messiah to be a supernatural person whose existence stretched back into the mists of ancient time.

THE ANSWER TO THE RIDDLE

If the Pharisees had tried to unlock Jesus' riddle by pondering the words of the prophets—and had they been willing to accept the implications of their thoughts—they just might have realized that the Messiah, the Son of David, was at the same time Isaiah's Everlasting Father "whose origins are from of old, from ancient times"!

And there's the answer to Jesus' riddle: David could call the Messiah his son, for the Christ would hail from his family line. At the same time, David could call the Messiah his lord, for the Christ would also be his God. This appears to be exactly what the Lord Himself tells us in Revelation 22:16, where he says, "I am the Root and the Offspring of David."

- Because Jesus is the *Offspring* of David, He is David's son.
- Because Jesus is the *Root* of David, He is David's lord.

One scholar writes, "Messiah as the 'Root of Jesse' (Isaiah 11:10) is not a sucker from the root but Himself the origin and strength of the Messianic line; 'the Root and the Offspring of David' (Revelation 5:5; 22:16) denotes Christ's divine-human nature as the source and descendant of David."[2]

Yet how can an answer to an ancient puzzle, even one as remarkable as this, bring life and vitality to our modern Christmas celebrations? How can the solution to a very old riddle bring us joy and satisfaction and wonder?

Had the Pharisees pondered *these* questions, they might never have missed the life that Jesus offered them.

WHAT DOES HE MEAN TO YOU?

Jesus wants His riddle to bring us much more than mere intellectual pleasure. Discovering the answers to other riddles may bring momentary fun, but God wants the answer to Jesus' puzzle to bring us infinitely more than that.

Have you ever pondered what it means to you—personally, individually, right at this moment—that your Savior, Jesus Christ, is "of old, from ancient times"? Have you ever stopped to imagine the staggering implications of His divine role as "the Alpha and the Omega, the First and the Last, the Beginning and the End" (Revelation 22:13)? Have you ever tried to grasp how much better your life is (and will be!) because Jesus is your Everlasting Father?

Understand that God's Word doesn't casually throw around the terms *everlasting* or *eternal*. While the Bible pairs these words with many *things*—everlasting *covenant,* everlasting *hills,* eternal *life,* for example—it uses those two words to describe only one *person:* namely, God Himself. God is often called everlasting or eternal (Genesis 21:33; Deuteronomy 33:27; Nehemiah 9:5; Romans 1:20). In one instance the Bible refers to "the eternal Spirit" (Hebrews 9:14), and once it speaks of the "Everlasting Father" in reference to Christ (Isaiah 9:6).

Think of it! Not even the angels are called everlasting or eternal. The Bible calls them "holy angels" or "destroying angels" or "powerful angels" or "elect angels"—but *never* everlasting or eternal. Among living beings, those two words are reserved for God alone.

And what difference should that make to us? Scripture leaves no doubt.

First, because Jesus is our Everlasting Father, He knows precisely how to reward us at the end of time (Revelation 22:12). The Alpha and the Omega knows every struggle you have ever faced. He has seen every problem that has ever come your way. He has stood with you during every challenge and hardship and triumph. What's more, because He is the *Everlasting* Father, He was there at the very beginning when your forefathers began your family line. Do you worry that you might get shortchanged in divine rewards simply because the gene pool of your family seems a bit shallow or the water a bit murky? Jesus is the perfect One to take all your family's long history into account, for He was there when the pool was first filled. This is why He could tell the startled Pharisees, who took such pride in their ancient lineage, "I tell you the truth, before Abraham was born, I am!" (John 8:58).

Jesus will make no mistakes when it comes time to hand out heavenly rewards. There is no chance that He will overlook some hidden deed or fail to take into account some obscure family weakness. Nor is there the slightest possibility that He will misjudge the proper size or number or character of the rewards to be handed out. As Everlasting Father, He knows all the quirks and traits of His sons and daughters, and He knows perfectly what rewards will best suit them. And because He is eternal, He has vast experience, gained through all of time, to guide Him in selecting exactly the right rewards for exactly the right individuals. No, Jesus will make no mistakes when it comes time to hand out heaven's rewards!

Second, because Jesus is our Everlasting Father, He knows exhaustively both all that has happened and all that will happen. He cannot be surprised by anything. That is why He tells John in the book of Revelation, "I, Jesus, have sent my angel to give you this testimony for the churches" (22:16). What testimony? The testimony detailed in the book, namely, "what you have seen, what is now and what will take place later" (1:19). "I will show you what must take place after this," John was told (4:1), and to make sure he didn't miss God's intent, at the end of the book an angel again tells him, "The Lord, the God of the spirits of the prophets, sent his angel to show his servants the things that must soon take place" (22:6).

When you know that you have a loving Father who knows the end from the beginning and everything in between, you can relax. The winter winds may howl and roar outside your door, and they may even tear off your roof and smash your windows—but you will remain safe within your house, even if the icy gale should seem to suck the breath right out of your body. As our Everlasting Father, Jesus can see everything that's ahead, and therefore He can confidently tell us how everything will turn out. That is what the Lord meant when, toward the end of His earthly ministry, He told His disciples to expect persecution and hardship, yet to look past these things to the glories to come. "You will be betrayed even by parents, brothers, relatives and friends, and they will put some of you to death," He predicted. "All men will hate you because of me. But not a hair of your head will perish" (Luke 21:16-18). Now, what exactly did He mean? You may be put to death, but not a hair of your head will perish? What good is *that?* Jesus meant that, because He knows the end from the beginning, no one can snatch His sons and daughters out of His hands (John 10:29). By standing firm in Him, He tells us, we will gain life (Luke 21:19). Only an Everlasting Father can make such a promise!

Third, as the source of all life, our Everlasting Father has the right and the power to give eternal life to all those who come to Him in faith. So He tells John, "Blessed are those who wash their robes, that they may have the right to the tree of life" (Revelation 22:14). As "the Lamb that was slain from the creation of the world" (Revelation 13:8), Jesus Christ knew from eternity past that He would offer Himself as the ransom for our sins. The cross was not some monstrous mistake, some unexpected satanic plot to frustrate God's will. Much to the contrary, "Herod and Pontius Pilate met together with the Gentiles and the people of Israel in this city [Jerusalem] to conspire against your holy servant Jesus, whom you [God] anointed. *They did what your power and will had decided beforehand should happen*" (Acts 4:27-28). Satan and his minions did only what God in His sovereignty had planned for them to do.

Because Jesus Christ is our Everlasting Father, He wants to give us the best life possible—and there's none better than eternal life with Him. *Nothing,* not even death, can frustrate His desire!

A RIDDLE TO MAKE US MERRY

Riddles have a long history of making our Christmas celebrations more merry. (How do sheep in Mexico say "Merry Christmas"? *Fleece Navidad!*)

Yet no riddle comes as close to giving us peace, assurance, and confidence as the one that Jesus asked the Pharisees so long ago. The answer to that riddle—our Everlasting Father Himself, not merely a correct string of words—can make your Christmas a time of unparalleled peace and rest.

It must have been that wonderful thought that, several centuries ago, inspired an unknown songwriter to pen one of our oldest Christmas carols. As you read again the familiar words, breathe a word of praise for your Everlasting Father. And be sure to thank Him because, by His grace, you are His beloved child.

> Of the Father's love begotten,
> Ere the worlds began to be,
> He is Alpha and Omega,
> He the source, the ending He,
> Of the things that are, that have been,
> And that future years shall see,
> Evermore and evermore![3]

S.H.

TWO

SEE ONE,
SEE THE OTHER

Anyone who has seen me has seen the Father.

All my life, I had wanted to visit the Big Apple. Once during high school I'd managed a visit to the Empire State, but I had never made it to New York City itself. Then, last year, my wife and I decided to take a short vacation to Manhattan. We made plans to visit the week after Thanksgiving, just as the city ramped up its Christmas celebrations.

We arrived in New York half an hour after First Lady Laura Bush and Mayor Rudy Giuliani flipped a switch to light up thirty thousand red, white, and blue bulbs on an eighty-one-foot Christmas spruce. Although the clock edged toward midnight by the time we reached our hotel, both Lisa and I wanted to begin our vacation with a glimpse of the famous tree. So we walked the few blocks to Rockefeller Center, swimming against a tide of one hundred thousand departing visitors who had gathered behind police barricades to watch the lighting ceremonies. We considered it a great way to begin our holiday adventure.

In the years preceding our trip, I had read a lot about New York City. I had seen countless images of the Manhattan skyline, of Times Square, and of the Empire State Building. I had talked with friends who worked in the city. Still, there's nothing like actually *being* there. Nothing substitutes for walking the city's bustling sidewalks, strolling through Central Park, marveling at the untold thousands of Christmas lights illuminating the Tavern on the Green, gazing at the festive holiday scenes in Macy's windows, doing a little shopping on Fifth Avenue, and getting your first taste of cannoli at a turn-of-the-century pastry shop in Little Italy.

Simply reading about the city or seeing familiar New York landmarks on television can't compare to a first-person experience. On a Sunday, Lisa and I decided to check out the famous Plaza Hotel, decked out in its elegant holiday finery—and we just happened to run into Mike Ditka, Jim Nantz, Randy Cross, and Jerry Glanville of CBS's *The NFL Today.* Honestly!

(Okay, to be *real* honest, we didn't physically run into them. But we did see them, in person, broadcasting live from an outdoor plaza across the street from the hotel.)

Our trip to New York City reminded me that if one really wants to get to know a place, nothing but a first-person experience will do.

And I think that goes double for getting to know an individual.

Up Close and Personal

Have you ever considered that Christmas is all about God giving us a firsthand experience of *Himself*? In the Old Testament, we first see God at work in the lives of several individuals and then in the life of a chosen nation. Yet it all seems a bit distant, a little third-person, as if we were viewing the Lord's activity through a telephoto lens.

Sure, we can hear the thunder and see the smoke atop a quivering Mount Sinai. We can watch as the *shekinah* glory fills Solomon's temple. We can weep as we observe fierce Babylonian soldiers slaughtering helpless Israelite men, women, and children. Yet where is God Himself? We see His hand everywhere, it seems, yet we never glimpse His face. And no wonder: Hadn't the Almighty told His servant Moses that "you cannot see my face, for no one may see me and live" (Exodus 33:20)? Little of what we see seems as personal as we'd like. Through the lens of the Old Testament, we feel awed by God's power and terrified by His holiness, and we remember that no one may casually draw near the burning Presence. But a *personal* God? Not exactly.

Then comes Christmas. Suddenly we see God's face… and He's smiling!

The Bible tells us that Jesus Christ came to earth to give us a first-person experience of God. He arrived that first Christmas so that we could see, hear, and touch the Almighty, up close and in person. Through Jesus, the God about whom we may only have read in the pages of the Torah, steps out of the Book and into our lives in a physical, touchable form.

"The Son is the radiance of God's glory and the exact representation of his being," says the writer to the Hebrews (1:3). Jesus "is the image of the invisible God," says the apostle Paul. "For God was pleased to have all his fullness dwell in him" (Colossians 1:15,19). At various times in His earthly ministry, Christ Himself told His disciples:

- "No one knows the Son except the Father, and no one knows the Father except the Son and those to whom the Son chooses to reveal him" (Matthew 11:27).
- "I and the Father are one" (John 10:30).
- "Know and understand that the Father is in me, and I in the Father" (John 10:38).

- "Anyone who has seen me has seen the Father" (John 14:9).

At Christmas, God arranged for us to get a first-person experience of Himself. No longer would we have to wonder what the Holy One of Israel was *really* like. No more would we have to learn of Him only through a telephoto lens. When Mary gave birth to Jesus at Bethlehem, God Himself came to live among us as Emmanuel, "God with us." Through our Everlasting Father, we can come to a personal knowledge of the heavenly Father.

So, then, what specifically can we learn about God the Father by pondering the earthly life of Jesus Christ? If Jesus came to reveal the Father, what exactly did He reveal?

A SHARPER PICTURE

First, we ought to realize that Jesus did *not* come to set aside the picture of God that we find in the Old Testament. Some folks have the mistaken notion that the God revealed in the Old Testament and the God described in the New Testament are two completely different deities. They aren't.

Jesus Himself said, "Do not think that I have come to abolish the Law or the Prophets; I have not come to abolish them but to fulfill them" (Matthew 5:17). Jesus did not come to overturn anything in the Old Testament, including its portrait of God. He came not to eradicate the ancient Hebrews' understanding of the Almighty, but to enlarge it and to color it in. He came not to replace, but to enhance.

When Lisa and I visited New York last Christmas, I didn't expect to find that Times Square actually looked like downtown Detroit, nor did I think I'd hear a lot of Polish spoken in Little Italy. My first trip to the Big Apple expanded my knowledge of and appreciation for the New York I had read about and seen on television, but it didn't eradicate the mental picture I already had. In the same way, Jesus came to fill out and sharpen our understanding of God, not to invalidate the divine picture already drawn by many Old Testament writers.

So how did our Lord fill out and sharpen our understanding of God? In what ways did His presence on earth broaden and enrich our picture of the heavenly Father? While these are questions worthy of a book all to themselves, let me suggest a few crucial areas in which our Everlasting Father, Jesus, expands our knowledge and appreciation of God the Father.

BIGGER THAN WE THOUGHT

Lisa and I had a wonderful time during our New York City visit. I learned things I had never known and enjoyed things

I had never experienced. My admiration for the city greatly increased.

But I also discovered something else during our trip: I knew a lot *less* about the city than I realized. It is much bigger and more interesting, and it harbors more surprises than I had ever dreamed.

What is true of New York City is likewise true of God. Although Jesus Christ reveals more of God to us than we could ever discover from the Old Testament alone—greatly enlarging our understanding of Him and enormously increasing our appreciation for His love and grace and power and holiness—we have only begun to scratch the surface of His majesty. The more we know, the more startled we are by what we *don't* know. Consider just a little of what Jesus teaches us about His Father.

We Are God's Children, and We Are His Unworthy Servants

The word *father* may reveal the biggest difference between the Old and New Testaments. Only in a few scattered places does the Old Testament use the term to refer to God, and never does it instruct anyone to pray to the Lord using that intimate name. But when Jesus comes on the scene, He explicitly tells His followers to address God with the unexpected words, "Our Father…" (Matthew 6:9). In an instant we know we have received a startling invitation to enter God's presence as dearly beloved children, as precious and favored members of His own holy family.

And yet not everything changes. This same Jesus tells a brief parable designed to remind us that, even though we are God's children, we remain in full-time service to the Eternal King. He ends one story by saying, "So you also, when you have done everything you were told to do, should say, 'We are unworthy servants; we have only done our duty'" (Luke 17:10).

The fact that God is our Father should never encourage us to forget that He is also our Lord. While Jesus explicitly called His disciples His "friends" (John 15:15), He also remained their "Lord" and "Teacher" (John 13:13). How do you suppose our Christmas celebrations might change if we more consciously honored both aspects of this truth?

God Has All Power, Yet Often Appears Powerless

Many times in His Judean ministry, Jesus exercised such overwhelming divine power that He frightened witnesses— even His own disciples. When He calmed a storm on the Sea of Galilee merely by telling the tempest to hush, Mark reports, "They were terrified and asked each other, 'Who is this? Even the wind and the waves obey him!'" (4:41). When He forced a legion of demons to depart from a tormented man, the villagers who knew the fellow's history were "afraid" and immediately began "to plead with Jesus to leave their region" (Mark 5:15,17). The day after Jesus cursed a fruitless fig tree on His way into Jerusalem, Peter saw the tree dried up from the roots and exclaimed, almost in disbelief, "Rabbi, look! The fig tree you cursed has withered!" (Mark 11:21). And when Jesus delayed going to the aid of his sick friend, Lazarus, some bitterly disappointed neighbors complained, "Could not he who opened the eyes of the blind man have kept this man from dying?" (John 11:37). People who knew Jesus knew that He commanded the miracle-working power of God.

And yet not everything changes. After all, Jesus reminded a stunned hometown crowd that, although many widows lived in Israel in Elijah's day, the prophet was sent to only one of them; and that, although many lepers lived in Elisha's day, only Naaman the Syrian was cured (Luke 4:24-27). The people did not like these reminders, and Matthew tells us that Jesus did not do many miracles in Nazareth (13:58).

We should remember, too, that Jesus Himself was born into this world in utter weakness, as a helpless infant. "He comes," writes Frederick Buechner, "in such a way that we can always turn Him down, as we could crack the baby's skull like an eggshell or nail Him up when He gets too big for that."[1]

Jesus reveals to us that the omnipotent God does not

always choose to use His power when and where and how we would like. And even when He does stretch out His almighty hand, He tends to frighten us. Jesus reminds us that we can give our heavenly Father no helpful advice on the best way to use His power and that it may break out where we least expect it and remain sheathed where we most count on it.

God Speaks Openly, and He Remains Silent

In Jesus, we have received the ultimate word from God about who He is and what He's like (Hebrews 1:2). Jesus explicitly tells us that "whatever the Father does the Son also does" (John 5:19) and "whatever I say is just what the Father has told me to say" (John 12:50). The common people loved hearing the Savior speak and often "were amazed at his teaching, because he taught as one who had authority, and not as their teachers of the law" (Matthew 7:28-29). Even to this day, we celebrate Jesus for using parables to make clear His delightful message. We rightfully rejoice that He wants people to know God as He truly is.

And yet not everything changes. Just as Isaiah acknowledged long before—"Truly you are a God who hides himself, O God and Savior of Israel" (45:15)—so Jesus sometimes makes His own message obscure. He told His disciples that, to those who have no real interest in applying His words, "I speak in parables, so that, 'though seeing, they may not see;

though hearing, they may not understand'" (Luke 8:10). When His unbelieving brothers urged Him to make a big splash at a religious festival in order to become more widely known, Jesus refused. John tells us, however, that, "after his brothers had left for the Feast, he went also, not publicly, but in secret" (John 7:10). When a pagan woman followed Jesus and His disciples for some time, pleading with Him to heal her daughter, "Jesus did not answer a word" (Matthew 15:23). And when our Lord appeared before His accusers shortly before His crucifixion, He kept silent before them and refused to answer their grim charges. His conduct irritated Herod (Luke 23:11), infuriated the religious leaders (Mark 14:63), and amazed Pilate (Matthew 27:14).

Our Everlasting Father shows us that while God loves to speak openly, He may also choose to remain silent. He who displays a gracious desire to reveal also demonstrates a sovereign willingness to conceal. Is it any wonder, then, that even in this magnificent day of post-Christmas grace, some of us struggle to know God's will?

God Invites Our Prayers, but He Resists Our Manipulations

Repeatedly in His ministry Jesus urged His followers to bring their requests to God in prayer. Often He gave them what amounted to a blank check: "If you remain in me and my words remain in you, ask whatever you wish, and it will be given you" (John 15:7; see also Matthew 17:20; 18:19; 21:22; Mark 11:23-24; Luke 17:6; John 14:13-14; 15:7,16; 16:23-24). Through His life and His teaching, Jesus demonstrated that God will always keep His promises.

And yet not everything changes. Jesus reemphasized that God cannot be manipulated into a box or put over a barrel. James and John once approached Jesus to ask Him "to do for us whatever we ask" (Mark 10:35)—a request that sounds, at least on the surface, very much like "ask whatever you wish, and it will be given you." James and John requested to sit on the right and the left of the Everlasting Father when He came into His glory. But Jesus told them, "to sit at my right or left is not for me to grant. These places belong to those for whom they have been prepared" (verse 40). Jesus refused to be manipulated, even by those closest to Him, and so He reminded us that God is no genie in a bottle, obligated to grant us our three wishes.

MORE TO SEE

In everything He did and said, Jesus expanded our understanding of God. When we gaze upon Him, we truly see the Lord.

Our Everlasting Father shows us that, while God is tender and compassionate, He also rules with a rod of iron. In one way, the Lord is absolutely predictable; in many other ways, He is full of surprises. Jesus shows us that God unwaveringly wants our best, but His idea of "best" often differs from our own.

Jesus Christ reveals His Father to an extent we could not have guessed—and yet in the showing we glimpse how much there is still to see.

S.H.

THREE

THE HEDGE

While I was with them, I protected them and kept them safe
by that name you gave me. None has been lost except the one
doomed to destruction so that Scripture would be fulfilled.

JOHN 17:12

*B*ob Reginald could hardly believe it. Things had
moved so *fast*. Yet he wondered even about that. It
seemed as though he had arrived only a few moments ago,
yet he knew he had been here for days, months, even years.
He shook his head and chuckled—a deep, sweet laugh that
came often to him in this place. Time really *did* have a totally
different flow in heaven than it did on earth!

As the accused shuffled into the courtroom, flanked by
stern bailiff-angels on either side, Bob reminded himself of
the grave responsibilities before him. It had never occurred to
him, as he had worked hour after hour in the automobile

factory back on Earth, that one day he would turn in his riveter for a judge's gavel. He had often read the apostle's words, of course, yet he never imagined that they would apply to *him*. As the scowling prisoner took his place at the witness stand, Bob's mind raced back to Paul's ancient prophecy:

> Do you not know that the saints will judge the world? And if you are to judge the world, are you not competent to judge trivial cases? Do you not know that we will judge angels? (1 Corinthians 6:2-3)

And now, here he was, *Judge* Bob Reginald of the Second District Court, Milky Way Division, getting ready to hear the case against one Malivious F. Grimmer. Bob picked up the legal brief that outlined heaven's case against M. F. Grimmer and quickly read the first few words.

Accused: Malivious Fang Grimmer

Occupation: Formerly a high-level tempter in the employ of Lucifer.

Charges:

Count One: Malivious Fang Grimmer is charged with unlawfully using his angelic powers to lure and entice God's elect into vile deeds unworthy of their divine pedigree.

Count Two: Malivious Fang Grimmer is charged with unlawfully using his angelic powers in

such a way as to inflict bodily and spiritual harm upon God's elect.

Count Three: Malivious Fang Grimmer is charged with
unlawfully using his angelic powers to
deceive God's elect into doubting the
goodness, grace, and love of the Sovereign
Lord.

These are weighty charges, Bob thought, but he knew that
even the demon now standing before him would soon admit
to their truth. In this courtroom there would be no question
of anyone lying or trying to deceive, for the King of kings
and Lord of lords had returned to earth in power and great
glory, ushering in His everlasting kingdom of peace and right-
eousness. Since it was impossible for anyone appearing in
His halls of justice to speak anything but the truth, witnesses
didn't need to swear to the accuracy of their testimony. The
glory of the Lord compelled all to testify to the unvarnished
truth, without the slightest trace of falsehood.

Bob already had presided over a number of these angelic trials, but today promised something special. Today he
would hear the case of the fallen angel who had dogged the
steps of the apostle Peter. Bob looked up and spotted Peter
in the gallery, patiently waiting to testify should he be called.
He appeared eager to learn a portion of his own untold
history.

Bob cleared his voice, sat up straight and tall behind his imposing bench, and banged his gavel.

"All rise in honor of the King of heaven!" called out a mighty angel, authoritative in voice and armed with a heavy broadsword. Everyone in the room instantly stood up, including Bob. The angel continued: "The Second District Court, Milky Way Division—the honorable Bob Reginald presiding—is now in session. May the truth of the Lord be declared. You may be seated."

Bob took his seat, along with everyone but the accused, and prepared to address the fallen angel. Just before he began, he noted that the demon seemed infinitely smaller and less imposing than he once imagined. At that moment he silently thanked God that, in the Resurrection, he had received a glorified body modeled after that of his risen Lord. No demon would look the least bit threatening to such a perfected soul.

"Malivious Fang Grimmer," the judge intoned, "do you understand the charges brought against you?"

Grimmer looked down at the floor and replied with a barely audible, "Yes-s-s-s."

"And how do you plead?"

The demon blanched. Sudden agony wrenched his body, and with gnarled, convulsive hands he gripped the railing surrounding the witness stand. For a moment it appeared as though he were trying to say, "Not guilty." Instead—much to his surprise and horror—all that came out was "Guilty as charged."

"Since you admit your guilt," Bob declared, "this court accepts your plea and will pass along a verdict of guilty to the Son of God, before whom you shall appear for sentencing. The function of this court hereinafter is to establish the character and extent of your offenses. The testimony heard this day shall be used as a basis for the judgment to be levied against you. Do you understand?"

Silence filled the courtroom, broken moments later by the fallen angel's hissed reply: "Yes-s-s-s."

Bob turned to the gallery and once again looked upon the man he knew as the apostle Peter. Bob had long considered Peter his favorite disciple, and he could hardly contain his excitement at having the Cephas of the Bible testify in his courtroom. Yet that time had come.

"Simon Peter," Bob announced, "this court summons you to the witness stand. Come forward and glorify your Lord!"

Peter rose swiftly and took his place at the stand opposite the convicted demon. Malivious tried to look his old victim in the eye but quickly found it a million times more comfortable to stare at the floor.

"Simon Peter," Bob continued, "this court has before it a summary of several events from your earthly life in which

Malivious F. Grimmer is alleged to have played a dark part. I will ask you to recount briefly what you know of each of these incidents. Then I will require Mr. Grimmer to divulge the details of his malevolent involvement. Are you ready to begin?"

"I am, Your Honor," Peter replied.

The demon stood silent, quivering, his dark eyes seemingly nailed to the floor.

"Would you tell this court about a time your Master healed your mother-in-law?" Bob asked.[1]

"Certainly," Peter answered. "I used to own a house in Capernaum. One day during a preaching trip, I and the other eleven came home with the Lord to find my mother-in-law sick in bed with a high fever. She had never been a particularly strong woman, and I could tell by my wife's worried looks that her mother might not be able to beat this fever. Before I could even ask the Master to help, He touched her hand, and the fever immediately left. Within moments, she felt well enough to get out of bed and serve us a wonderful dinner. We were all amazed!"

"Mr. Grimmer," Bob said, "what part did you play in this incident?"

Once more it seemed as though the fallen angel tried to say one thing while his lips insisted on speaking another. For a few moments, he could manage only a few gurgles and rasps. But then his head jerked back, as if yanked by an unseen hand, his nervous eyes stared dully toward the judge's bench, and he slowly admitted his part in the matter.

"It…was *I*…who…made the wretched woman sick," he declared at last, and then the words came tumbling out. "I admit it: For long years I enjoyed great success in the spiritual realm by wreaking havoc in the physical realm. And I nearly had this man's wife convinced that"—here he stopped and darted his eyes upward as if at some potent, yet invisible observer—"*He* couldn't possibly care for them. If He did, then why would her mother be sick? Why would her husband be traipsing all over the countryside, leaving her alone to care for their children? I just about had her, and him with her, and then"—his voice dropped to a low growl—"the *Holy One of God* barged in and destroyed all my hard work."

"What do you mean?" the judge asked.

"You heard him!" Malivious snarled. "The One they worship touched her hand and healed her. He was always protecting them, even when the fools didn't know it." And then his raspy voice fell silent once more.

Judge Reginald used the silence to study some notes, and then he addressed Simon Peter.

"Peter," he said, "now would you tell us about two incidents that occurred on the Sea of Galilee? I believe you know the ones to which I refer."[2]

"I do, Your Honor," the former fisherman replied. "In the first incident, Jesus and I and the other disciples were in a boat, rowing toward the land of the Gadarenes. A sudden storm swept over us, violent and unexpected, and we thought we were all going to drown. Somehow the Master was sleeping through all of it, and we shook Him awake to ask whether He cared that we were all about to die. He calmly got up and said, 'Quiet! Be still!' to the *storm*—and everything instantly grew still. We didn't yet understand who He really was, and it terrified us.

"Then, a little later, we went sailing again. This time, Jesus didn't accompany us; He told us He'd see us on the other side of the lake (how He'd manage that, we didn't know). Again a storm came up, and although we strained all night at the oars, we couldn't get anywhere against the wind and the waves. It looked bad—and then we saw something that looked even worse. A ghost appeared to be gliding over the waves toward us! Just then, the Master Himself called out, and I knew the "ghost" was really Jesus. So I asked Him to bid me come to Him on the water. He agreed, and I stepped out of the boat and onto the waves. I walked toward my Lord, and I *loved* it! But for some reason I stopped looking at Jesus and instead started noticing the waves, which seemed bigger than ever. I started to sink. I had time only to shout, 'Lord, save me!' And before I knew it, I felt the Master's hand pulling me to safety."

"Thank you, Simon," Bob said. Turning to the evil spirit, he commanded, "Now, Mr. Grimmer, tell us what happened from your perspective."

The demon did not try to speak lies this time but angrily resigned himself to hearing the horrible truth from his own wicked mouth.

"I tried to drown all of them," he sneered. "You might be surprised to learn how many 'accidents' and 'acts of...*Him*...' were really examples of our work. 'If you can't turn 'em, burn 'em,' we used to say. But time after time, *He* intervened. He kept protecting them, shielding them from our strongest blows. The first time on the lake, He used words we couldn't oppose; the second time, He used a hand we couldn't resist. The fools never even knew how safe they really were."

Peter sighed when he heard the fallen angel's testimony, a sigh of wonder, not of remorse or regret. He had long since come to rely on the protecting hand of Jesus; nevertheless, it felt good to hear how close He had always been.

Judge Reginald interrupted Peter's reverie with yet another request. "Simon Peter," he said, "would you now tell this court a little about that night when the enemies of our Lord arrested Him in the garden?"[3]

At this Peter grew quiet, and his hand instinctively went to his chin as if to stroke a beard long vanished. At length he began his story.

"Shortly after we celebrated the Passover seder," Peter recalled, "our Lord said something that both hurt and puzzled me. 'Simon, Simon,' He said, 'Satan has asked to sift you as wheat. But I have prayed for you, Simon, that your faith may not fail. And when you have turned back, strengthen your brothers.'

"*Turn back?* I didn't know what He meant, and I pridefully replied that I would never leave Him, that I would even die for Him. He answered—sadly, I know now—that within hours, I would deny three times that I ever knew Him. Oh, how foolish and arrogant I was not to believe Him!

"Later, we went, as usual, to the Garden of Gethsemane—but this was no usual night. He asked James and John and me to pray with Him, but such a dreadful heaviness fell on all three of us that we drifted off to sleep, leaving Him alone. Almost before we could rub the sleep from our eyes, a band of angry men appeared out of the blackness. When they tried to arrest the Master, I drew my sword and cut off the ear of one of them. I felt awake enough to fight! But Jesus rebuked me and said, 'Put your sword away! Shall I not drink the cup the Father has given Me?' And then He stooped to pick up the severed ear, gently placed it back where it belonged, and healed the man. I didn't know what else to do—so I ran away.

"I do not like to remember what happened next, but perhaps it is enough to admit that I did indeed deny my Master three times, just as He had said. The third time I did it, a rooster crowed, and in the distance I saw my dear Lord turn toward me and look straight into my eyes. At that moment I burst into tears and fled into the night. It's a wonder I didn't die along with Him that night."

"A 'wonder.' Bah!" growled the demon, who didn't wait for an order to give his side of things. "Yes, we asked to sift you like wheat. But your Master prayed for you, and we could never get fully inside that hedge! It was I who caused your eyes to grow heavy that night in the garden, but still His prayers kept me from doing all the damage I had planned. It was I who suggested you remove that young man's head with your sword—but you are such a clumsy bungler that all you could manage was to lop off an ear. And when *He* stepped in to heal the little rat, He kept the mob from tearing you limb from limb. You didn't know that, did you? Even when He looked at you in the courtyard, after you freely denied Him (with my prompting, of course) and you broke down like a bawling little baby—you didn't know that *even then* He was protecting you, did you? We nearly had you then! Just a few more steps, a few more seconds, and you would have been tripping blindly after our friend, Judas, down the steep path to hell.

"But that *look!* I can see it still, and I loathe it still. He has more ways of protecting you than you know, and even though we trained you to despise many of His methods, He protects you regardless. I wish I had never seen any of you!"

A deep quiet reverberated through the room—one born of reverence and thanksgiving to God, not of sorrow or sadness—and for a good while no one spoke. But soon the questions resumed, and by session's end the record showed many more ways in which the Lord Jesus Christ had consistently foiled the lethal work of Malivious Fang Grimmer and all his evil cohorts. Many in the courtroom audience laughed when they heard the apostle Peter's description of his angel-engineered break from prison.[4] Others wept for joy when they learned some additional details regarding the old fisherman's restoration after an early morning breakfast on a quiet beach.[5]

And everyone—with the notable exception of Malivious Fang Grimmer—left the courtroom that day with a deeper love for Jesus Christ, the Lover of their souls. Not that they needed the kind of testimony they heard that day! Still, all left the heavenly courtroom bursting with praise for their Everlasting Father, the One who had, in countless ways, wrapped His protective arms around them during their days on earth.

S.H.

FOUR

THE OPEN VAULT

Ask and it will be given to you; seek and you will find; knock and the door will be opened to you. For everyone who asks receives; he who seeks finds; and to him who knocks, the door will be opened.

MATTHEW 7:7-8

Do you ever find it difficult to accept nice gifts at Christmas? When you tear off the wrapping paper, do you ever hesitate for a moment, hoping your response pays unspoken dividends to the giver? Many of us feel obliged to "do something" to justify our receipt of gifts, whether that means acting more excited than we really are or reciprocating with a gift of equal or greater value.

We may have the same feeling in response to God's gift of Jesus. The benevolence of Jesus flows from His love for us. But we don't work to repay God's grace or to earn our keep in the house of our Everlasting Father. Instead, the work we do flows out of hearts filled with gratitude. When we forget that the grace and gifts of our Everlasting Father can come to us both freely and often, we cheat ourselves. In a spiritual sense, Christmas comes every day to Christ's sons and daughters, bringing new and exciting blessings.

Yet Jesus tells us that to access those blessings, we need a key.

THE KEY TO HEAVEN'S TREASURES

An old Scottish legend tells how a little shepherd boy was walking through the fields one day when he discovered a rare and beautiful flower. He bent down, carefully picked it, and held it in his hand for just a moment.

As he lifted the flower to his nose to smell its sweet fragrance, he heard a distant rumbling. At that moment the side of a nearby mountain lifted up, as if it were on oiled hinges—revealing a king's ransom. Huge piles of gold, silver, rubies, sapphires, and diamonds littered the mountain floor.

Slowly and with great trepidation, the boy entered the hollowed-out mountainside and dropped the flower inside the vault. He gazed upon all the precious stones and other treasures and then anxiously reached down to pick up a handful of diamonds and rare jewels. As he turned to walk out of the vault, a voice said, "Don't forget the best."

The frightened boy looked around and thought, *Well, I think I have picked out the most valuable things.* He turned to walk out again, and once more the voice counseled him, "Don't forget the best." The lad hesitated but hurried out of the cave. Immediately he heard another rumble, and the mountain slammed shut. And one last time the voice boomed, "Don't forget the best—the flower you left inside."

At that moment all the boy's jewels turned to dust. He really had forgotten the best: the flower, the key to the vault.

Now imagine the vault of your Everlasting Father. What might it contain? The Bible says that we will find everything inside that we need for this life—and more beside. We will come upon sapphires of encouragement for when we grow discouraged. There will be diamonds of endurance to help us withstand the temptations of this world. We will discover earthly treasures such as houses, cars, and collectibles that He allows us to enjoy. His vault contains all that He desires to give us, the tangible as well as the intangible. Does not Jesus Christ, our Everlasting Father, own everything (Hebrews 1:2)? None of us owns anything that was not first given to us by our Savior. But like any earthly father who gives gifts to his children, can't our Everlasting Father also take them away?

Yet more than any earthly dad, our Everlasting Father stockpiles a heavenly storehouse that overflows with good things. But so often we lose sight of all that Christ desires to give us. How do we gain access to our Lord's vault? How do we get the mountain to open for us?

When Jesus spoke from atop a mountain one day, He revealed to us the key for the door of His amazing generosity. Matthew 7:7-8 tells us that the key to our Everlasting Father's vault is the sweet flower of prayer: "Ask and it will be given to you; seek and you will find; knock and the door will be opened to you. For everyone who asks receives; he who seeks finds; and to him who knocks, the door will be opened."

Jesus told the multitudes and His own disciples that the key to accessing the breathtaking generosity of their Everlasting Father is to ask, seek, and knock. We do this asking, seeking, and knocking through prayer. But to many of us, prayer does not seem like a precious flower. It does not seem like much of a key. So we do not pray.

Perhaps we don't feel the need. Perhaps we have prayed, and it seems that nothing has happened. Or perhaps as we draw close to Jesus in prayer, we feel ashamed. We mistakenly believe that our sin makes us unworthy to receive fine gifts from our Everlasting Father, and so we do not ask for them.

THE VAULT OF GOOD GIFTS

Jesus wants us to take full advantage of His generosity. But if we are to personally access the fullness of that gracious liberality, the Bible tells us to pray "continually" (1 Thessalonians 5:17). The words of Jesus in Matthew 7:7 might more literally be translated, "Ask and keep on asking; seek and keep on seeking; knock and keep on knocking." Persistent prayer is the key to the limitless vaults of heaven.

To encourage us to understand and take advantage of His boundless generosity, Jesus asks us, "Which of you, if his son asks for bread, will give him a stone? Or if he asks for a fish, will give him a snake? If you, then, though you are evil, know how to give good gifts to your children, how much more will your Father in heaven give good gifts to those who ask him!" (Matthew 7:9-11).

Our Lord reminds us here that, even though earthly fathers are imperfect and inconsistent in their giving, they still desire good gifts for their children. If that is true, then how much more is it true of our Everlasting Father, who *delights* in giving good gifts! Jesus assures us that He has a vault filled to overflowing and that *everything* in His vault is good.

It is because Jesus wants to give us only good gifts that we shouldn't be surprised when He doesn't always answer our prayers in the affirmative. I have to admit that I have prayed for some ridiculous things, items that I never should have requested. Since Christ has a vault filled only with good things, however, and because the thing I asked for wasn't in the vault, He had to tell me no. He refused to give me a stone—even one as pretty as a diamond—when what I really needed was bread. How grateful I am that the vaults of the Everlasting Father contain nothing but good gifts!

As we continually come before Him—asking, seeking, and knocking—Jesus has promised to give us His good gifts. When we ask, He gives. The Everlasting Father says to you and to me, "I am always here with you and everything that is Mine is yours."

Can you imagine Christmas in the household of our Savior? Imagine waking up one Christmas and looking under the tree. Beneath those spreading branches you find one gift, then another, and another, and you keep seeing *your* name on every one of those tags—all from your Everlasting Father. Everything He has, He shares with us.

THE PERFECT GIFT

While Christ has mountains of good gifts for us, He came that first Christmas to give us the ultimate gift, the perfect gift. Our Everlasting Father came to seek and to save those who are lost—those lost in a lifestyle of immorality, those lost in a sea of ungratefulness, those lost in a thick fog of confusion. In other words, He came to seek and save *us*. He Himself is His perfect gift to you and to me.

And just what makes a gift "perfect"? What are the characteristics of a perfect gift?

The perfect gift has two primary traits: It always expresses the personality of the giver, and it unfailingly meets the needs of the receiver. Any gift that meets those two criteria can indeed be said to be *perfect*.

I remember one Christmas many years ago when one of my longtime friends gave my oldest son, Ed, a towel with his name on it. Now, Ed was about eight years old. What does an eight-year-old boy need with a monogrammed towel? The gift certainly expressed my friend's personality, but it did not come close to meeting my son's needs. So was it a perfect gift? Hardly.

On another Christmas, a different friend gave his wife a shotgun—and she *hates* hunting. Again, the gift expressed his personality but most definitely did not meet her needs.

Our Everlasting Father never makes that kind of mistake, nor did He on that first Christmas. He left the side of His Heavenly Father, came down to be born into the human family, and dwelt among us. And when He grew up, He gave His life for the remission for our sins, thereby meeting our deepest need: to be forgiven of our sin. It was a perfect gift: It not only expressed the personality of the Giver, but it also met the deepest needs of the receivers. Jesus' gift of Himself was the ultimate, perfect gift. And it still is.

IS HE YOUR DADDY?

One Christmas season seemed colder than usual. The temperature had dropped to three or four degrees, and little white flakes fell softly. A man driving down a deserted street noticed a young boy, about seven or eight years old, huddled alongside a building. *How strange,* he thought. *What is such a young boy doing out in this bitter cold?*

The man quickly drove up to the boy and stopped his car. He rolled down his window and asked, "Son, is everything all right? You need to get out of the cold! You'll freeze to death out here."

"I ca-ca-can't, sir," the boy replied through chattering teeth.

Puzzled by such an answer, the man stepped out of his car to speak with the boy face to face. He could see that the youngster had been crying. "Look, son," he said, "I'll take you home. Are you lost? What's the matter?"

"Mister," the boy replied, "I *can't* go home."

"Sure, you can go home," the man answered. "Where do you live?"

"I live right up there," said the boy, pointing to the second floor of an apartment building behind him.

Now even more confused, the man told the boy, "Well, son, get out of the weather and run home."

"You don't *understand*," the boy replied. "My daddy gave me five dollars and told me to come down here to this store. He gave me a list of things to buy. When I tried to cross the street, the wind was blowing and I was so frozen with cold that somehow the money blew right out of my hand. Now I can't find it. I've looked everywhere."

"Well, just go home and tell your dad what happened," the man counseled. "He'll understand."

"Mister, you don't know my daddy," answered the boy. "He has been drinking, and he's mean all the time. He is especially mean tonight. If I go up there and tell him I lost that five dollars and didn't get what he wanted, he will get real mad. I don't know what he'll do."

With his heart breaking, the man reached into his wallet and said tenderly, "I'll lend you the money, son. Take this five dollars." He then ushered the little guy into the convenience store and helped him get some bread, milk, and a few other items. The cost came to a little more than four dollars. The clerk handed the change to the boy.

"Now, son," he said, "you take that change and run on home. Don't say anything to your daddy about it. Just give him what he wanted."

"Thank you," the boy said, suddenly grinning. He started back across the street while the man watched. Before the Good Samaritan could hop back into his car, the boy stopped, turned around, and ran back across the street. Throwing his arms around the man's legs in a tight hug, the boy exclaimed, "I wish *you* were my daddy!" Then the youngster spun around, ran back to his doorway, and bounded up the steps to his apartment.

Do you know what the man did then? Before he went home, he drove around three or four more blocks looking for another boy who just might have lost a five-dollar bill.

This Christmas, Jesus Christ, the Everlasting Father, is looking to give *you* a five-dollar bill. He knows what you've lost; He knows what you most require; and He yearns to give you the perfect gift, the one that satisfies your deepest longings and meets your deepest needs. Most of all, He wants to be your real Daddy...forever.

GIVE HIM YOURSELF

Christmas usually involves the exchange of gifts. So this year, what can we give to our Everlasting Father? How can we best respond to the priceless gift of Himself?

A little boy was asking himself exactly that question one Christmas. "Mom," he said, "it's Jesus' birthday, but I haven't gotten Him anything. I *get* gifts and I *give* gifts, but I've never *given* anything to Jesus—and it's *His* birthday. This year I want to give a gift to Jesus. What can I give Him?"

"Well, honey," the mother replied, "what do you want to give Jesus?"

The boy thought hard for a moment and said, "I think I would like to give Him something really valuable. Could I give him something made out of gold?"

"I don't think He needs that," his mother answered. "Remember, the streets of heaven are paved with gold."

The boy realized his mother was right, so he thought some more. But no matter how hard he thought, he couldn't come up with anything better than gold. "Mom," he said finally, "what *can* I give Him? What in the world can I give Him?"

"Honey," she replied tenderly, "there's nothing in the world we can give Him because He's got the whole world in His hands. He made it and put it all together."

Her words caused a sudden light to shine in the little fellow's eyes, and he cried out, "Then maybe I could give him the moon and the stars!" But as soon as he said it, he saw a new problem and added sadly, "No, I guess they're His too. What *can* I give Him?"

The boy's wise mother sat down next to her son, wrapped her arms snugly around him, and put her kind face next to his. "There's only one thing you can give Him that He doesn't have Himself," she said, "and that's *you*."

This Christmas, give Jesus *yourself*. It's the perfect gift for the Everlasting Father who already has everything else.

E.Y.

FIVE

TIDINGS OF COMFORT AND JOY

Therefore, since we have so great a cloud of witnesses surrounding us, let us also lay aside every encumbrance, and the sin which so easily entangles us, and let us run with endurance the race that is set before us.... For consider Him who has endured such hostility by sinners against Himself, so that you will not grow weary and lose heart.

HEBREWS 12:1,3 (NASB)

On August 3, 1992, eight men were competing in the first semifinal heat of the four-hundred-meter run at the Barcelona Olympics. The first four runners to cross the finish line would advance to the final to be held two days later. Among this talented group of runners was Derek Redmond, a leading contender for the gold medal.

The gun sounded and the runners were off. In lane five

Derek neared the halfway point when, suddenly, his right hamstring popped. Intense pain flashed through his leg, and he fell down on the track.

All hopes of a medal vanished in an instant. But Derek refused to give up. If he couldn't have the medal, at least he wanted the finish line. He limped painfully toward the finish line—but could he manage even that? It looked doubtful.

Suddenly a determined man pushed through the crowd, passed a surprised security team, and ran onto the track. The man was Derek's father, who came alongside his son and spoke words of assurance and encouragement as Derek struggled down the long homestretch. Millions of television viewers around the world joined the stadium crowd in cheering father and son as, together, they finished the final meters of the race.

Most us can't remember who won that race or even who eventually won the gold medal. But few can forget Derek Redmond and his dad. They finished the race together.

GOOD FATHERS ENCOURAGE

Good fathers know how to encourage their children—and they'll surmount any obstacle, overcome any difficulty, just to fill the hearts of their discouraged sons or daughters with "tidings of comfort and joy."

And at Christmas encouragement is precisely what some of us need. This time of the year, which is supposed to be filled with "peace on earth, goodwill toward men," sometimes has just the opposite effect on us. Perhaps we have lost a job. Maybe we are facing relocation to another city, uprooting our family and moving across the country. Or it could be that a slow economy means fewer Christmas presents this year for family and friends, and we feel blue because Christmas will not be as "big" as in the past.

For others of us, the discouragement may be as simple as fighting the Christmas rush. Traffic is heavy, parking looks impossible, and lines seem endless. We haven't yet put up the tree, and we can't find the one present that Billy or Megan has requested. (I get discouraged just thinking about it!)

Sometimes we feel more discouraged during this special season than at almost any other time of the year. Our most memorable moments seem to occur at Christmas. And now those fond childhood memories, those special loved ones, and the friends who have moved away are present reminders of the emptiness that has been created in their absence. Now is when we most need the encouragement of Jesus Christ, our Everlasting Father.

The apostle Paul knew this well, so he wrote to some struggling Christian friends in the city of Thessalonica: "May our Lord Jesus Christ himself and God our Father, who loved us and by his grace gave us *eternal encouragement* and good hope, *encourage your hearts* and strengthen you in every good deed and word" (2 Thessalonians 2:16-17). How appropriate that God's Word should remind us that our Everlasting Father gives His children "*eternal* encouragement"! Jesus Christ wants to greatly encourage us this Christmas season.

DISCOURAGEMENT IN ANCIENT ROME

In a different time and a different season, the Christians in Rome faced great discouragement. They lived and worshiped the one true God in a city of decadence, immorality, and cruelty. Many were losing their lives in Rome's coliseum because of their faith in Jesus Christ. The author of Hebrews wrote to these downhearted believers to remind them (and us) of the eternal encouragement found in their Everlasting Father. Interestingly, he chose a setting much like that of Derek Redmond's Olympic race to frame his encouraging words.

Picture yourself at a track meet in a coliseum or stadium, the writer to the Hebrews says. In the stands on every side sits a great cloud of witnesses, a sea of faces too numerous to count.

Who are these witnesses? They are those who have participated in the race of life, just as we are running today. The "cloud of witnesses" especially includes those listed in Hebrews 11, men and women of history who demonstrated great faith in God despite hardships and opposition. All of these witnesses continue to cheer loudly—for *us*.

I can almost hear them yelling their encouragement.

Moses, staff in hand, is shouting, "You may feel cornered by a hostile army behind you and a great sea in front of you, but God's power will see you through! Keep on keeping on!"

I can hear Gideon saying, "You may be outnumbered, but you can still be victorious. Stay in your lane! Keep running!"

Samson is among them, loudly declaring, "You may be caught in a sin that will scar you for the rest of your life, but God wants to use you again!"

Rahab, the former prostitute, is calling out, "You may have sold yourself into immorality, but your God is a God of second chances!"

I hear David speaking, "You may be guilty of adultery or even murder, but God is going to honor and bless you if you seek His face. Keep running!"

Can you hear the encouragement of these faithful brothers and sisters in Christ? Can you see how their lives are meant to give us strength today? They are part of a great cloud of witnesses surrounding you, cheering you on. There's the faithful pastor of the church where you grew up. Over there stands your Great-aunt Esther, who prayed for you every day. And down a couple of rows sits your old Sunday school teacher or neighbor or grandfather or friend, folks who used to put their arms around you and gently lift your chin to heaven. "Keep looking up!" you hear them say.

Did you know that the Greek word for "witness" can also be translated "martyr"? The enthusiastic folks in these stands are not mere spectators. They are aggressive participants in the race of life, spiritual athletes who have gone before us. They have been right where you and I are, and they all are shouting encouragement.

Yet none of them, as great as they are, has tickets for the VIP box. That place of honor is reserved for just one Witness, a standout performer who has cheered for every athlete who has ever run the race, even for every winner now sitting in the stands. He is cheering for us more enthusiastically and continuously than anyone has ever done before. He is the Encourager of encouragers.

His name is Jesus Christ, the Everlasting Father.

But how does Jesus encourage us? you may wonder. Derek Redmond's dad came running out of the stands to put his arm around his hurting son's shoulder and help him shuffle to the finish line. How can Jesus do *that?* Our Everlasting Father no longer walks the earth physically as He once did, so how can He continue to encourage us?

Sometimes our Lord does so through His dear children, as the apostle Paul reminds us: "For you know that we dealt with each of you as a father deals with his own children, encouraging, comforting and urging you to live lives worthy of God, who calls you into his kingdom and glory" (1 Thessalonians 2:11-12). Perhaps there is someone in your life, right now, who longs to put his or her arm around you in an act of comfort and encouragement. Consider those arms the tender embrace of Jesus.

Sometimes Jesus encourages us through remarkable events and answers to prayer that come together at just the right time. This happened often when Jesus walked among us: "People were overwhelmed with amazement. 'He has done everything well,' they said. 'He even makes the deaf hear and the mute speak'" (Mark 7:37). We can feel greatly encouraged when we see Jesus stretch out His mighty hand and overwhelm us with amazement.

Sometimes our Lord encourages us by fulfilling the promises of His Word, by bringing to pass amazing events just as He prophesied them: "I foretold the former things long ago, my mouth announced them and I made them known; then suddenly I acted, and they came to pass" (Isaiah 48:3).

Sometimes, when we feel so weary we cannot even walk, Jesus picks us up and carries us to the Promised Land, though we may be too blind with weariness to see: "You saw how the LORD your God carried you, as a father carries his son, all the way you went until you reached this place" (Deuteronomy 1:31).

How does our Everlasting Father encourage us? In more ways than we can count, at more times than we can see, in more places than we can know.

LAY ASIDE EVERY ENCUMBRANCE

And yet, despite this stream of divine encouragement, we sometimes stumble. We hit a rough patch of track and pop a hamstring, tripping over encumbrances and sins that cause us to stumble and fall. And many of us take some pretty nasty tumbles right around Christmastime.

What are encumbrances? They could be those activities, places, or people with whom we associate that, while not wrong in themselves, are not in our best interest. They may keep us from realizing our full potential as spiritual athletes. They may impair our judgment and hinder our discipline. Jesus calls us to put them aside.

He also calls us to get rid of those sins that so easily entangle us. What are these "besetting sins"? Besetting sins are the attitudes, habits, or secret areas of life that we have been wrestling with for a long, long time. They are those sins that keep coming back to plague us and push us down.

Like any good father, Jesus works in our lives to test us, discipline us, and move us beyond our encumbrances and besetting sins. He does not stop encouraging us when we stumble. He keeps on encouraging us to righteous living. One way He does so is through the Bible, a record of His teachings and an account of His life. In His Word He provides us with a complete record of the stumbling blocks and pitfalls in the race of life, as well as the means by which we may overcome them.

Can you think of a better time than Christmas to begin laying aside those encumbrances and focus anew on running a race that is pleasing to the Lord? Christmas marks the end of the year—the perfect time for us to look back and evaluate how successfully we reached the goals and objectives we set earlier in the year. Christmas is also a time to look ahead to the new year, a time to lay aside those things that cause us to stumble.

May I ask, What is it about your life this past year that has prevented you from reaching your full potential in Christ? What has prevented you from running with endurance? And what would it take to lay these things aside? If Jesus were to speak with you face to face at this very moment, in what ways do you think He would encourage you?

No Need to Pretend

A professional basketball coach named Cotton Fitzsimmons was trying to encourage his team, which was then suffering through a long losing streak. In a pregame pep talk, he decided to give his guys some encouragement built around the word *pretend.*

He gathered his players in the locker room and said, "Guys, I want you to pretend that you're not at the bottom of the league, but at the top. I want you to pretend that you're not on a losing streak of twelve games, but on a winning streak. I also want you to pretend that this game is not just a regular-season game, but a play-off game that will lead to the championship. Now go out and *beat* these guys!"

The team went out, played four quarters, and got thrashed by the Boston Celtics. After the game, the players could see their coach's deep discouragement. One player put his arm around the dejected leader and said, "Coach, cheer up. Pretend we won."

In the race of life, there is no need to pretend. Our Everlasting Father is running with us. He is with us at the start of the race, and He stands at the finish line, encouraging us along the way not to give up. He runs alongside us, and at times He even carries us across the finish line!

We live the victorious Christian life and successfully run

the race of faith because we are in Christ Jesus and because He lives within us. He gives us the encouragement and the endurance we need to finish the race. With Him, we do not have to grow weary or lose heart.

Jesus promises us that we will never again be alone. Even if we feel abandoned and lonely this Christmas, our Everlasting Father stands beside us, helping us run the race despite whatever injury we have suffered. He calls out to us to keep on keeping on, for we *can* make it to the finish line—with His help.

Listen for His Voice

A talented little boy was taking piano lessons. His mother knew he had much potential, and his teacher thought the boy might really become "someone" someday.

Yet, over time, the boy grew tired of the piano. He kept doing his scales and chords, but he wanted to quit. About that time it was announced that Ignacy Paderewski, the famous concert pianist, was coming to their city, and the boy's mother thought that taking her son to the performance might encourage him.

Finally the big day came. A large crowd gathered in the auditorium, waiting for the master. While expectant ticket holders talked and milled around, this little boy wandered innocently onto the stage. Ignoring the crowd, he stepped up to the beautiful, black grand piano and started to play "Chopsticks." He had forgotten some of it, but he continued to practice and play despite his lapses. Finally some chagrined concertgoers tried to coerce him offstage. Two or three even booed him, but the little boy continued to play the tune.

Paderewski observed what was taking place and, quietly but dramatically, made his way onstage and stood behind the boy. The great pianist put his arms around the boy as he played, and suddenly the two began to play beautiful music, part of a famous concerto. The music astonished the crowd. While Paderewski played, he continued to whisper into the boy's ear, *"Don't stop. Keep playing. Don't quit. That's right, keep going. Never stop!"*

Sometimes when we want to quit, the Everlasting Father, like Paderewski, is right there with His arms around us, telling us, "Don't stop! Keep going!"

Do you hear the magnificent voice of Jesus Christ this Christmas season? Can you hear His encouragement? Whatever your challenges might be, however the crowd around you might be trying to discourage you or even coerce you off the stage, listen instead to the whispered encouragements of your Savior. Cock your ears and heed the supportive words of both those who have gone before you and those who stand with you now.

And remember this: Jesus stands above them all, encouraging you in His own almighty way to keep heading toward the finish line. He has saved a spot in the winner's circle just for you.

E.Y.

SIX

JUST AS HE SAID

The angel said to the women, "Do not be afraid, for I know that you are looking for Jesus, who was crucified. He is not here; he has risen, just as he said."

MATTHEW 28:5-6

I don't know, Salome. I just don't know what to think anymore," said Mary to her dear friend. "All my life I've longed to have a man in my life who would keep his promises to me. No, don't look at me like that! I don't mean a lover or even a husband. I mean a trustworthy man who would do for me exactly what he said he'd do. I thought we had found such a man. But now...I just don't know."

Mary buried her face in the shoulder of her devoted friend and wept quietly for several long moments. Salome said nothing, but stroked Mary's long, dark hair while softly embracing her. At length Mary straightened up again, brushed the tears from her eyes, and reviewed the wrenching events of the previous few days.

"Salome," she began again, "how are we to believe He can keep His promises to us *when He's dead?*"

This time Salome reached out her long, slender hand and gently cupped her friend's wet chin. "Tell me what you mean," she said.

"What I *mean?*" Mary replied, sniffling. "You know as well as I do what I mean. You heard His promises just as I did, and you know He kept all of them, until—" She stopped short.

"Yes, I know them," Salome replied. "But I want to hear about them from you, the way you remember them. Would you do this for me? It may be all we have left."

Mary nodded, wiped away more tears as they rolled down her cheeks, and tried to compose herself. Her mind drifted back to a scene that had taken place about two years before, although now it seemed much longer ago. Despite her deep sorrow and confusion, a smile tugged at the corners of her mouth.

"I can't even say for sure when I first saw His face," she said, trying to peer through mists of memory. "All I really remember is a thick darkness and a feeling of rage and confusion that kept my heart aching and my spirit empty. I did and said unspeakable things, horrible things, and those who didn't run away from me drove me away from them. And then one day, out of the fog, I heard a voice speaking—a male voice, strong and clear. Unlike the others, it sounded full of love, not fear or revulsion. One part of me thrilled to the voice, while another part felt consumed by hatred and terror. I heard myself shrieking profane words and felt myself clawing at the air.

"And yet the Person did not draw back or recoil in disgust. Rather, I heard His voice grow in power as it commanded 'evil spirits' to leave me at once—and the next thing I knew, I found myself lying on the ground. The mist had lifted, I could see and hear clearly, and at that very moment I saw His face: kind, gentle, understanding, yet filled with a might and an authority beyond my imagination. Then He took my hand, bid me rise, and instructed those present to give me something to eat."

Smiles had returned to both women, and Salome quietly added, "You could hardly believe it later when we told you that Jesus of Nazareth had cast not one, not two, but *seven* demons out of you!"[1]

"I can barely believe it still," Mary replied. "My life to that point had hardly seemed worth living: I felt constantly alone, constantly rejected, constantly wracked with a raging hunger and thirst, not only of body, but of spirit. Then the Master came—and in one moment He made me whole!

From then on, I stayed as close to Him as possible. I could not hear enough of His words or see enough of His work. I counted it a great privilege to help support His ministry out of what little money I had.[2] Before long, I did not doubt that the One who had healed me *had* to be the Holy One of Israel, the very Son of God Himself."

"So we all thought," Salome said quietly. "And yet, now…how could it be? He lies dead in a tomb. His disciples have scattered like chaff in the wind. And His promises? They died with Him on the cross."

Mary nodded in silent agreement, yet her heart yearned for a far different ending. Suddenly she felt compelled to recount the promises He *had* kept. If her friend were right—and she saw no way that she could be wrong—the only thing they had left was the memory of promises fulfilled.

"I remember, as if it were yesterday, one of the first promises I heard Him speak," Mary said. "Do you remember, Salome? I think you were with Him at that time too. From prison, John the Baptizer sent some of his disciples to the Master to ask whether He really was the Messiah. Things hadn't turned out as John had expected. Jesus told them to report what they had seen Him do: give sight to the blind, cause the lame to walk, heal the lepers, open the ears of the deaf, even raise the dead. Who else could He be but the Messiah?

"He thanked His Father for hiding the truth from the

wise and powerful and revealing it instead to 'little children.' Oh, Salome, I knew that *I* was one of the 'children' He meant! And then He gave a beautiful promise, a promise that meant the world to me, coming as I did from a place where I never felt the slightest peace or rest. Do you remember? He said, 'Come to me, all you who are weary and burdened, and I will give you rest. Take my yoke upon you and learn from me, for I am gentle and humble in heart, and you will find rest for your souls.'"[3]

"Yes, I remember that too," Salome said. "They were beautiful words."

"Oh, but you know they were more than words!" Mary replied. "Just a little later, we and thousands of others followed Jesus to a remote place in the country. We wanted to hear from Him so badly that most of us forgot to bring along any food. It looked as if we would all go hungry—and then you know what happened!"

"It was a miracle," Salome said, as if in a dream.

"Nothing like it had ever been seen in Israel!" Mary cried. "Why, He took five barley loaves and two fish, and somehow made them swell into enough to feed *thousands!*"

"I heard there were five thousand men alone, plus all of us women and children," Salome recalled.

"And then He did it again just a little while later," Mary said.

"Four thousand men that time," Salome added.

"You always had a head for numbers," Mary laughed. "But don't you see how those two miracles fulfilled His promise? He said He'd give us rest, and He did. He told us to take our weariness and our burdens to Him so that He could lift them from our shoulders—and He did! Do you know, Salome, that, when the demons plagued me for all those terrible years, I never had a moment's rest? Do you know how weary I had become? Yet I'm sure He understood my agony, for with my own ears I heard Him say, 'When an evil spirit comes out of a man, it goes through arid places *seeking rest and does not find it.*'[4] But in Him, Salome—in Him!—I found my rest. Even in the arid place where He fed us all with a few loaves and a couple of fish, I found my rest."

Salome nodded, stood up, and turned toward the window. The thick curtain of night appeared to be lifting at last, and she knew that in just a little while the sun would peek over the drab Judean hills. What would they find, she wondered, when she and Mary visited the tomb? For that they hoped to do.

"I am glad to hear that story again," Salome said, "yet I cannot help but wonder, Mary: How weary are we at this moment? How rested do we feel? It is wonderful to remember the old promises Jesus kept, but what of His promises for the future? Surely you have not forgotten those."

Mary's shoulders sagged, and though her eyes looked down to the floor, the images they sought seemed much further away. Her mind groped to understand, but understanding eluded her.

"It is as I said, Salome," Mary replied. "I don't know. I just don't know. I remember His promises as well as you do. He declared, 'For the Son of Man is going to come in his Father's glory with his angels, and then he will reward each person according to what he has done.'⁵ But how can a dead man come anywhere, let alone in 'glory'? How can a dead man reward anyone? He kept so many of His other promises that I had no doubt He would keep that one, too. But now…"

Salome turned suddenly from the window and sat down opposite her friend. She still had every intention of following through on their plan to visit the tomb and anoint Jesus' body—although she doubted it would do any good. A huge stone sealed the entrance to the grave, and a guard of soldiers had been posted to keep "their kind" out—and Salome didn't want her friend to hope for anything, well, *foolish*. While their Lord's arrest and crucifixion had taken everyone by surprise and had effectively crushed their hopes, Mary had taken the news especially hard. As much as anyone, she had *believed* in this man. She believed He meant every word He said—and Salome did not want her to fall back into her old lifestyle when it became clear that things would never return to what had been. So before they walked to the tomb in the early morning rays of the sun, she wanted to remind Mary that their Teacher had also made some darker promises.

"Mary," she began, "I know that you loved our Lord. We all did. And I know you thought that, in Him, you had found a man whose word you could trust. But I also think that, in light of what has happened, you need to remember some of His other promises."

"What do you mean?" Mary asked, startled at the sudden change in tone.

"I mean that we ought to recall some of His promises that seemed a little darker than the others, and harder to understand. Not everything was lilies and sunshine, Mary."

Mary looked at her friend, searching for some sign of hope. Seeing none, she dropped her gaze and said nothing.

"Mary," Salome began, "do you recall what the Master said about the reason for His coming? 'I have come to bring fire on the earth,' He said. 'Do you think I came to bring peace on earth? No, I tell you, but division. From now on there will be five in one family divided against each other, three against two and two against three. They will be divided, father against son and son against father.'[6] Mary, that is not a promise that we liked to hear, but it is a promise nonetheless. And it seems to have come to pass, even among the Twelve. You heard that Judas hanged himself?"

Mary nodded, but remained silent. Again, quietly, she wept.

Salome continued. "Mary, you speak of promises, but you must remember the harsh along with the pleasant. You know, as well as I do, that He spoke of one promise more than He did of any other."

"But what could it *mean?*" Mary cried out, full of emotion. She stood to her feet. "I thought that if we refused to speak of it, it would not take place. None of us understood it, but it sounded horrible, horrible—too horrible to be true."

"And yet it was a promise, a promise of *His,*" Salome replied gently. "He said it many times and in many ways. He said, 'For as Jonah was three days and three nights in the belly of a huge fish, so the Son of Man will be three days and three nights in the heart of the earth.'[7] And he said, 'We are going up to Jerusalem, and the Son of Man will be betrayed to the chief priests and the teachers of the law. They will condemn him to death and will turn him over to the Gentiles to be mocked and flogged and crucified. On the third day he will be raised to life!'[8] Mary, those, too, are promises, although none of us understood what He meant."

This time, it was Mary's turn to stare out the window, noting how the light had begun to wash over the hillsides.

She made no reply, but instead turned to inspect the spices that she and Salome had prepared for their trip to the tomb.

"Do you not wish to accompany me to the grave then?" she asked dully.

"Oh, Mary, you know I do!" Salome replied. "I loved Him, as you did. I love Him still. I just do not want your heart to break more than it has." She paused and then touched her friend's arm. "Come. We will speak no more of this. Let us gather the spices and go. It is time."

The two women silently gathered the burial spices and then trudged off through a waking town toward the tomb where earlier they had seen some men lay the body of Jesus. Neither had the least notion of what awaited them.

As they rounded a corner, pure and dazzling light blasted their eyes. A mighty angel of God, in white clothes more brilliant than the noonday sun, sat alone atop the rolled-away stone. His overwhelming presence so alarmed and startled the women that they dropped their spices on the ground and froze in place, petrified. The angel immediately greeted them and, in a voice like rolling thunder, declared, "Do not be afraid, for I know that you are looking for Jesus, who was crucified. He is not here; he has risen, just as he said."[9]

At that moment, the world stopped for Mary. She heard almost nothing else the angel said. Her mind seized upon four words, blessed words, tiny words that poured infinite hope into her shriveled soul: *just as He said.*

Could it be true? But how could it be? And yet how could the word of an angel safely be doubted? It *had* to be true! And if so, the "dark promise" that Salome had only just repeated actually shone like lightning! The Lord's followers may not have understood His promise, but Mary's Lord had indeed kept His word. *Just as He said!*

Robbed of speech, the two women fled from the tomb, their hearts bursting with joy and terror. Joy, for the news of their living Lord. And terror, for heaven had broken into their world, bathing it in fearful light.

As she ran, Mary's delirious heart told her that there could no longer be any doubt: She really had met a man whose every word could be trusted. The news was *not* too good to be true! No, she knew this news was so true that it outstripped all the good she would ever know.

S.H.

SEVEN

MEASURING THE IMMEASURABLE

I pray that you, being rooted and established in love, may have power, together with all the saints, to grasp how wide and long and high and deep is the love of Christ.

hristmas was only a week away. The Simmons family had decorated the tree, set out the Christmas candles, and carefully placed the porcelain Nativity scene on the hearth. This was to be the first Christmas for their newborn child, Billy.

But all was not well.

Little Billy developed colic and often fell sick. His frequent ill health demanded a lot of attention from Mom and

Dad, and that meant the Simmons's other two children, Tommy and Mary, received less attention than normal.

Tommy was then about five, and he quickly grew jealous of the baby. In the evenings, Tommy would compete with baby Billy for the attention of his dad. It bothered him that everybody seemed to be talking about baby Billy: "Let's see the baby," "The baby is so cute," and "Make sure the baby's out of the draft!"

Tommy desperately wanted part of the love, so he took to standing on his head and doing flips—yet nobody seemed to notice. Still Tommy tried to grab some love. In the middle of the night, when Dad got up to help Mom with Billy, Tommy also got up, anxious to seize part of the action.

One evening while Dad held the baby, Tommy once again started standing on his head, starved for his dad's attention. Of course, the father knew he had a problem. As he looked at the Nativity scene and glanced at the Christmas candles, an idea came to him.

Ah, he thought, *maybe I can explain it to Tommy like this.*

He called Tommy over, took a match, and lit the large Christmas candle in the center of the arrangement.

"Tommy," he began, "see this large candle? This is your father—this is me. And see the light from the candle? This light is my love."

Tommy became quiet and very interested. Next his dad

lit the smaller candle on the right and said, "See that candle there—that's you. When you were born, I gave all of my love to you. But look—my candle is still burning! I gave all of my love to you, but I still have that love. I didn't lose any."

He lit a third candle and continued, "Then Mary was born, and I gave all of my love to her, too."

He paused, then finally lit a fourth candle.

"And now I am giving Billy this same love," he declared.

With four candles now burning brightly, he said tenderly to his son, "You have all of Dad's love. Mary has all of Dad's love. And now Billy does too. But look! I have plenty of love left. Now, Tommy, do you understand?"

Tommy thought for a moment and, with a sigh of relief and peace said, "*Phewww,* boy! Oh, Dad, I think I understand. Love is something that never gets used up."

The next night, the father waited for Tommy to come running in and return to his old antics. But that night Tommy slept soundly because he finally understood that real love never gets used up.

MEASURING THE IMMEASURABLE

If you try to measure the love of Christ, you will find yourself trying to measure the immeasurable. How do you grasp the immeasurable love of our Everlasting Father? None of us can fully explain the love of Christ. But where can we begin?

I think we begin with John 3:16, where Jesus says, "For God so loved the world that he gave his one and only Son, that whoever believes in him shall not perish but have eternal life." Not only do we see our heavenly Father demonstrate immeasurable love in giving us His only Son, but we also see the immeasurable love of Jesus, our Everlasting Father, who willingly gave Himself for us.

Then perhaps we could move to Ephesians 3:17-18, where Paul tries to explain the love of Christ. He puts down physical dimensions that help us in our scientific age to graphically picture this transcendent truth: "I pray that you…grasp how wide and long and high and deep is the love of Christ."

If we were to merge Ephesians 3:17-19 with the tremendous self-declaration of Christ in John 3:16, we might find a framework in which to attempt to measure the immeasurable. Perhaps then we could hear our Everlasting Father say, "For *I* so loved the world that *I* gave *Myself,* that whoever believes in *Me* shall not perish but have eternal life." In so doing, Jesus gives us some concrete pictures for our understanding.

Jesus says to you and to me, "For I so loved the world"— that is the *width* of His love.

He says, "That I gave Myself"—that is the *length* of His love.

"That whoever believes in Me"—that is the *depth* of His love.

"…shall not perish but have eternal life"—that is the *height* of His love.

Now maybe we can get a little better handle on Christ's staggering love for us.

THE WIDTH OF CHRIST'S LOVE

How wide is the love of the Everlasting Father? The love of Christ is worldwide. His love is unending and immeasurable. It doesn't exclude anybody—high or low, rich or poor. His love does not discriminate by color, creed, or nationality. It's handmade, personalized just for you and for me. And for that reason, it's worth remembering for all time.

In 1878, British archeologists unearthed an obelisk—a slender piece of granite covered with hieroglyphics—from beneath the sands of Egypt. By deciphering the ancient symbols, scholars discovered a civilization that no one then living knew anything about. They named the obelisk "Cleopatra's Needle" and took it to London, eventually erecting it by the Thames River.

Prior to its placement, a group of English citizens decided

to construct a time vault to be placed beneath the obelisk. If London were to fall into ruins in the distant future, they reasoned, this time vault would provide a record of the nineteenth-century city. So they set about gathering a London telephone directory, a newspaper, some clothing, and some toys. They also decided to choose an item representing the religious life of the era and appointed a committee to select a single sentence from the Bible to be placed in the vault.

If you had been on that committee, what verse would you have recommended? What holy text would you consider the Mount Everest of biblical revelation? For most of us, the task probably doesn't seem so difficult. No doubt we would choose the verse that we learn first and forget last. We would select the verse that has been translated into nearly every known language and dialect. The verse explains itself, yet carries a meaning so profound that we can never fully comprehend it. Read it aloud now as though you had never heard it before:

> For God so loved the world that he gave his one and
> only Son, that whoever believes in him shall not perish
> but have eternal life. (John 3:16)

This is, indeed, the Mount Everest of Scripture, with a width so vast it girdles the planet. "Greater love has no one than this, that he lay down his life for his friends," said Jesus to His disciples (John 15:13), and yet He was willing to lay down His life not only for His friends but also for those who beat Him and spat upon Him and mocked Him and crucified Him. Jesus freely laid down His life for His enemies, that through His shed blood He might make them His friends forever.

Only supernatural love can enable a person to lay down one's own life for an enemy. And we *were* enemies of Jesus Christ when He died for us. The Bible tells us, "But God demonstrates His own love toward us, in that while we were yet sinners, Christ died for us" (Romans 5:8, NASB). Even though we remained estranged from Him, blasphemed Him, and shamed Him in our immorality, He died for us.

How impossibly wide is the love of our Everlasting Father!

THE LENGTH OF HIS LOVE

For as long as I can remember, the biggest shopping day of the year has been the day after Thanksgiving. Folks madly run around buying Christmas presents, planning meals, and looking for that perfect tree—and before long, the price of Christmas adds up.

I thought having a wife and three sons was expensive at Christmastime. Now I have my wife, three sons, their wives, and seven grandchildren. I can speak from experience—Christmas is *costly!* But consider the price Jesus paid to make us right before God and have a personal relationship with us. He went as far as one could go—giving His own life. The real reason for Christmas is not His birth, but His death. Jesus Christ died on our behalf to make us right with God.

We have Adam to thank for this world that is so estranged from God. After he disobeyed God in the Garden of Eden, Adam passed along a sinful nature to all his progeny. We inherited that inborn compulsion to sin, but we can't do business with a Holy God if we are not holy ourselves. None of us have the moral, physical, or spiritual capacity to get right with God on our own. Therefore, Jesus died on a cross for your sin and mine so that we could get right with God. Our Savior faced the punishment that we so rightly deserved, enduring the full weight of pain, hurt, and suffering caused by our sin.

Jesus died on our behalf, purely out of love. Now that's both divine and supernatural! And it's immeasurable because His life carries no price tag.

THE DEPTH OF HIS LOVE

The depth of Christ's love is revealed in two simple words: *whoever believes.* The Everlasting Father desires a relationship with *anybody* who will believe in Him. The depth of Christ's loves extends to all the sin-forsaken orphans of this world, offering us adoption into the family of God.

Have you ever read the classified section of your newspaper? If so, perhaps you've seen the section labeled "Adoptions." Every week I read of couples offering to adopt newborns. One ad read, *California-doctor dad, at-home mom wish to adopt newborn. Will provide love, security, and opportunity. Call Steve and Elaine.* Another read, *Financially secure couple, with happy two-year-old daughter in Georgia, want a baby boy or girl to complete their loving family. Phone Hillary or Terry.*

This Christmas season, the Everlasting Father has placed an ad in His paper (unlimited circulation!) inviting all who are estranged from Him to come and join His heavenly family. But there is one condition, summarized by those two special words: *whoever believes.*

The New Testament contains thirty-five passages declaring that salvation consists of having faith in Jesus Christ. Faith is an act of the whole individual, not merely one's intellect or emotions. Real faith begins when we believe that Jesus died to atone for our sins and that we can receive His forgiveness. The atoning work of Christ is sufficient for all who believe in Him. That is the depth of His love.

Jesus' invitation to salvation originates from the throne room of heaven and reaches through time and space to the deepest part of our being. His offer appeals to our deepest needs, known by no other. It is extended to the least expected and the most unlikely—that is, even to you and to me.

This Christmas, many will be singing that well-known carol "Away in a Manger." But many more will be living and saying, "Away *with* the manger!" Some believe and some do not—but Christ's offer remains open for *whoever believes,* for anyone who wants the abundance He has to give. Have you trusted in Him and experienced the depth of His love?

THE HEIGHT OF HIS LOVE

If the Everlasting Father were to join you this Christmas, what gift do you imagine He would have for you under the tree? Would it be the annual bonus you've been praying to receive? Could it be that new computer you hoped to get? Perhaps it is that new pair of shoes you saw in the store. If you had asked the Lord for His greatest gift, what would it be?

The greatest gift your Father can give you is *life!* His gift of life has both quantity and quality—it's abundant, and it's everlasting. Jesus Christ so loved the world that He gave Himself, that whoever believes in Him *shall not perish but have everlasting life.* Everlasting life demonstrates the height of His love. It carries us ever up, lifting us to the heavenly places and securing our place in the family of God.

Yet this Christmas many of us may second-guess our security in Christ. Perhaps this past year has not been all that great. Some of us keep looking at the mistakes and sins we committed in the last twelve months, which is preventing us from enjoying the assurance of His gift of everlasting life. What a tragedy!

Paul wanted to spare us such agony, and so he asked, "Who shall separate us from the love of Christ?… For I am convinced that neither death, nor life, nor angels, nor principalities, nor things present, nor things to come, nor powers, nor height, nor depth, nor any other created thing, shall be able to separate us from the love of God, which is in Christ Jesus our Lord" (Romans 8:35,38-39, NASB).

Once we are "in Christ," Paul assures us, *nothing* can separate us from the love of Jesus. Not life. Not death. Not the future. Not the past. *Nothing.*

Do you know any love wider, longer, deeper, or higher than the love of your Everlasting Father?

THE MEASURE OF
HIS IMMEASURABLE LOVE

In the Middle Ages, a popular monk announced one Sunday morning, "Tonight in the cathedral, I'm going to preach a sermon on the love of the Christ." The news spread and multitudes came, sitting and waiting in the silence of the vast house of worship.

The late afternoon sunlight, shining through the brilliant windows, slowly dissipated until the room grew dark. Eager men and women continued to sit, stand, and wait to hear the much-anticipated sermon. Finally the monk walked out to the altar and lit a single candle on the candelabra. Quietly he took the candle and stepped to the center of the cathedral, where a tall cross with a statue of the body of Christ stood.

Without saying a word, the monk took the candle and held it to illuminate the feet of Jesus. He paused for a moment and then held the candle to the Lord's side, again without saying a word. Then he took the candle to each of the Lord's hands. Finally, he held the candle to the thorn-crowned brow.

And that was his sermon.

How did the people react? They cried. They sobbed. They wept openly because they knew they had been ushered into the presence of a mystery far beyond their intellectual and spiritual scope.

When we stand before the cross this Christmas, we don't say, "I wonder how tall it is." We don't say, "I wonder how long its arms are." We don't say, "I wonder how much that cross weighs." No, when we stand before the cross, we know that the cross is tall enough to reach heaven. The arms of the cross are wide enough to include sinners like you and me. And the cross weighs enough to tip the scales of mercy and grace in our favor.

This Christmas when we stand before the cross, we can understand a little more of the width, the length, the depth, and the height of our Everlasting Father's love for us. Through the long years of time, He continues to smile and say to each of us, "For I so loved the world that I gave Myself, that whoever believes in Me shall not perish but have eternal life."

This Christmas, when you see candles burning—whether at a candlelight service, at a party, or in your own home— know that an everlasting flame burns bright in the heart of the Savior...just for you.

E.Y.

EIGHT

WITH US ALL THE TIME

Immediately Jesus reached out his hand and caught him. "You of little faith," he said, "why did you doubt?"

MATTHEW 14:31

During no other holiday of the year does our culture accept and accommodate Christ more than at Christmas. Nativity scenes appear in homes and businesses. Stores and shopping malls play classic, Christ-centered Christmas carols. Christmas pageants draw curious crowds to church.

Yet with all the external evidences of the Christian faith, many people still harbor doubts about the nature and character of Jesus Christ. Several years ago when the pop group Emerson, Lake & Palmer pondered how the trappings of Christmas often don't match up to its reality, the band recorded a cynical number called "I Believe in Father Christmas." The song implies that the nativity of Christ amounts to nothing more than a fairy story.

This nagging voice of doubt has whispered in the ears of men and women since the days of Adam and Eve, and it continues to call into question our beliefs about God. Even Jesus' disciples fell victim to doubt.

THE STORMS OF LIFE

Of all people, Peter—whose name means "rock"—doubted his Everlasting Father. His faith in Jesus wavered one stormy night on the Sea of Galilee as he attempted to join his Lord for a late-night stroll on the water.

This particular battle with doubt occurred while Peter and the other disciples toiled on the lake, all alone. Earlier in the day Jesus had sent them ahead in the boat while He climbed a mountain to pray. Before long, a violent storm whipped over snow-capped Mount Hermon, its howling winds descending rapidly down the Jordan River Valley before sweeping over the sea. After rowing for eight or nine hours against gigantic waves, the disciples had managed to travel only two or three miles.

By the fourth watch of the night—around 3 A.M.—they had grown tired and discouraged. They had little to show for a night of fighting the storm, yet the Bible makes it clear that, somehow, they still were right in the middle of God's will. Jesus had known all along that His men were going to battle that storm, yet He sent them into its teeth.

Do you know that Jesus still does things this way? Sometimes He sends us smack into the middle of a late-night howler—even at Christmastime. We expect calm seas and a light breeze, but instead we find ourselves facing a gale that appears ready to capsize the whole ship.

I wonder—could you be fighting a storm at this moment?

The Bible describes at least two kinds of "storms" that toss us violently upon life's wild waves. First, there is the storm of correction. Remember Jonah? When he wandered outside of God's will, the Lord sent a storm to shake him up. God intended to use the frightening tempest to correct him and lead him back to the right road. The Lord also uses storms of perfection, in His wisdom directing howling winds to stretch us and test our faithfulness to God.

We shouldn't consider God's methods unusual, for good earthly fathers often employ their own storms. If you're a parent, consider how often you have let your children experience the storms of life in order to help them grow and mature into adulthood. In the same way, the Everlasting Father sometimes uses storms to test our faith and to build our confidence in His provision. And sometimes those storms bluster and blow at Christmas. When hurricanes rage in our lives, we almost can't help but wonder, *Where is God? How could this have happened? How can I trust Him when the waves are so high?*

A SIGHT TO BEHOLD

In the midst of the nasty storm that rained upon the Sea of Galilee, the disciples thought they saw a man walking on the water, as if he were riding the crest of a wave. When out of the haze and the rain they saw a human shape, they cried out in fear, supposing they saw a ghost. But this was no ghost; it was the Everlasting Father Himself, Jesus Christ.

"Take courage!" He called out. "It is I. Don't be afraid" (Matthew 14:27).

Isn't that just like a father? Assuring his frightened children that their daddy had come and would not abandon them?

Years ago Dr. Neal Littleford and his son, Mark, went fishing in Alaska. Neal had often promised his son that the two of them would make the trip, and now Mark was twelve years old. Once they were in Alaska, they took a little pontoon plane to a lake in an otherwise inaccessible area, accompanied by the pilot and another man.

That first day they fished but caught nothing. "I know where we'll go," said the pilot, and the next day the party flew into another bay. "The salmon are coming in," he told his passengers. "We're going to catch fish here."

Boy, was he right! As soon as the hooks hit the water, the fish began tackling each other to get on the line. It was an exciting day as everyone caught salmon left and right.

At the end of a great day of fishing, the group returned to the plane. But they immediately realized they had forgotten something. A twenty-three-foot tide flows in and out of that bay. The tide was out, and their plane was now sitting on rocks. Since they couldn't take off without water to provide a runway for the pontoons, they decided to spend the night. They cooked their fish and enjoyed a beautiful night under the stars.

The next morning the tide had come back in, so they packed the plane and took off. Within seconds they realized that one of the pontoons had cracked open and filled with water. The extra weight caused the airborne plane to rock and gyrate over the icy water before crashing into the arctic bay.

All four survived the crash. The pilot and the other man, both strong swimmers, made it easily to shore. Dr. Littleford likewise could have made it to shore, but not without leaving Mark behind. His young son wasn't yet physically strong enough to overcome the riptide. As the two survivors watched helplessly from shore, they saw a heroic father stay with his frightened boy in that frigid arctic water until both father and son disappeared beneath the waves. Dr. Littleford and Mark died of hypothermia.

When I first heard this story, I thought about it for a long time. I asked myself, *What would I have done had I been that father?* Understand, I'm not particularly the heroic type. *What would I have done?* It didn't take long to decide that I would have stayed with my boys. And I don't think I'm very unusual. I believe that virtually *every* father would do exactly what Dr. Neal Littleford did that day.

Why? Because good fathers refuse to abandon their children. They will stay with them even to the end. Perhaps they cannot always save their sons and daughters from death, but they can save them from the fear of perishing alone.

Peter made this very discovery, and far more, that night on the Sea of Galilee. After he realized that the approaching figure was no ghost but his beloved Lord, he recovered his wits and asked hopefully, "Lord, if it is You, command me to come to You on the water."

"Come," Jesus replied. With that assurance, Peter immediately climbed out of the boat and began to walk toward Jesus on the water.

Now Peter was no fool. He knew that what he was doing made no earthly sense. As a seasoned fisherman, Peter had often sailed the Sea of Galilee; he felt at home on its familiar waters. And every day before, after returning to shore with a nice catch of fish, Peter had stepped out of the boat and either touched bottom or started to swim.

But not this time!

Can you imagine what Peter might have been thinking the moment his feet touched the water, but didn't sink beneath the surface? And can you imagine the thoughts of the other disciples? No doubt Peter suddenly wished that Jesus had said more than "Come." Surely he wished for a promise: "Come, *and everything is going to be fine.*" Yet even without such an assurance, Peter had exercised genuine faith (if only a little), and Jesus honored him for it.

FIXING OUR EYES ON JESUS

Peter looked to Jesus and, like a son taking his first wobbly steps toward his father, began to walk on the waves. And as long as Peter kept his eyes on the Master, he remained safe and secure. With his gaze fixed on his Everlasting Father, the space between him and his Lord became peaceful and calm, as tranquil as the eye of a hurricane.

Do you know what happens in the eye of a hurricane? Not much; the area remains quiet and absolutely tranquil. One can look up and see through a perfectly clear sky all the way to the heavens. Peace reigns in the eye of a storm. There, in the eye of a vicious storm so long ago, Peter felt sure of his safety...but only as long as he kept his eyes fixed upon his Everlasting Father.

I heard recently about one little boy who discovered the amazing strength to be found in keeping his eyes fixed on his dad. The lad had grown critically ill, and his doctors ordered a very dangerous surgery. The boy's father entered his son's room to sit at his bedside and tell his fearful child of the impending operation. "Dad," his son responded, "I will stay here at the hospital and have the operation—*if* you will stay with me. I want you to stay with me all the time."

"Of course I will stay with you," his father assured him.

A few days later, the boy spent six hours in the operating room. The first thing he saw upon regaining consciousness was the face of his father, filled with calm assurance. Seeing it, he closed his eyes again and went back to sleep. A few more hours passed, and the lad once more opened his eyes. Again he saw the face of his father.

"This is the greatest day of my life!" he exclaimed.

"Son," the father replied softly, "it *can't* be your greatest day. You're in the hospital."

"Oh no, Dad, it *is* the greatest day of my life," answered the son, "because you've been with me all the time!"

Even in the storms of life, we can know the assurance of Christ's presence and protection when we fix our eyes on Him. Our loving heavenly Father stays with us through everything. "Surely I am with you always, to the very end of the age," He promised (Matthew 28:20). And He never breaks His promises.

DOUBTING YOUR DOUBTS

In many ways, Christmas itself can become a stormy season that tempts us to doubt the character and goodness of God and to turn our eyes away from the Everlasting Father.

Some of us may be tempted to doubt His provision when we cannot provide gifts for our own children. Others of us may doubt God's love when we feel forgotten at Christmastime. I have known a few to doubt God's protection when the pretty lights of the season have accidentally set their house afire. Christmas has its shares of storms, and keeping our eyes upon Jesus during the season is not always easy. Yet it's crucial, as Peter reminds us.

We need to remember that Peter had at least enough genuine faith to leave the boat and step out onto the turbulent waters. He knew who controlled the water and who was walking on the sea, inviting him to come. So he took one step, then another...until something happened.

Peter took his eyes off Jesus.

In one terrifying moment, the apostle saw the gale-force winds and the huge whitecaps crashing around him. Fear gripped his heart, and he began to sink. Have you ever wondered how far down he went before he cried out for help? Did he sink knee-deep? Waist-deep? How far did he go?

How far do *you* have to sink before you call out to God? If this Christmas you feel as if you are sinking in doubt and despair, don't wait until you hit the sea floor to call out to Jesus Christ. Set your eyes upon Him, and He will save you.

Peter learned this lesson the hard way. "Lord, save me!" he cried. And what happened? "Immediately Jesus stretched out His hand and took hold of him, and said to him, 'O you of little faith, why did you doubt?'" (Matthew 14:31, NASB).

What is doubt? Doubt is not the same as unbelief, although doubt certainly may lead to unbelief. Rather, doubt is the nagging voice in the back of your mind calling into question the very core of your beliefs.

In the context of Scripture, doubt is not necessarily a bad thing. Doubt either leads us to deeper faith or deeper despair. Galileo said, "Doubt is the father of discovery." Writer Frederick Beuchner calls doubt the "ants in the pants of faith." Our Everlasting Father is a God of light and truth, and we needn't leave our inquiring minds in the vestibule in order to worship Him.

Where do our doubts come from? Generally, two kinds of doubts assail us.

Intellectual doubts most often stem from our lack of

Bible knowledge and a wrong understanding of God. Too often we listen to our culture's twisted commentary on God and lose sight of the truth of His Word. To keep our eyes upon the Everlasting Father means to stand unwaveringly on His promises and His principles.

Emotional doubts, on the other hand, often arise from disobedience. When we lose sight of our purpose, doubt comes calling. While our standing before God remains secure, we begin to lose the assurance of our salvation. Before long, this type of doubt debilitates us and renders us ineffective in Kingdom service. It is this kind of doubt that assailed Peter before he reached out for his Savior's hand; it is this kind of doubt that almost cost him his life.

What should we do when we find ourselves doubting God? Before anything else, we should realize that we are not alone. Abraham, the individual the Bible calls "the man of faith" (Genesis 12–13; Galatians 3:9); Gideon (Judges 6:33–7:11); the disciple Thomas (John 20:24-29)—all of these men and many others sparred with doubt. Doubts come to all of us, but we need to deal with our doubts without allowing them to dominate and rob us of our faith.

So *how* are we to deal with doubt? I like what Martin Luther once said: "You cannot keep the birds from flying over your head, but you can keep them from building a nest in your hair." I would say the same about doubts. We must deal with them one at a time, à la carte. First we must recognize our doubts. Then we must test them against the truths of God's Word, asking: "What does God reveal about Himself? What does God say about us and our role in the situation?" When we embrace and act upon those great truths, we will begin to doubt our doubts and believe our beliefs. Our doubts will dissipate, and our faith will grow.

TAKING HIS HAND

Peter survived his battle with doubt, but only because the Everlasting Father stretched out His hand to pull him to safety. Could it be that some of us are waiting this Christmas for Christ to reach down and pull *us* out of the wild waves? When we're sinking, looking to Jesus is the only rational thing to do!

Yet not everyone reaches out a hand in response to His. Don't be like Judas Iscariot, who failed to properly deal with his doubts. When things turned out differently than he expected, he took his eyes off Jesus and began looking in the mirror. At that moment he began sinking in the waters of greed. Soon he sold out Jesus for a few measly coins. Why didn't he wait until Easter? Why didn't he stick around until Pentecost or until Paul came on the scene? Had he waited, he would not have become the scoundrel of the ages that he is.

Are you wrestling with doubt this Christmas? Has your focus on the waves and the wind and the rain of your life diverted your attention from the Savior? If so, reach out and take His hand. Your Everlasting Father has promised to guide you and lead you through your doubts and uncertainties. As your strong and loving Father, He makes promises to you that He fully intends to keep. As your trustworthy Father, He constantly reminds you that you are His child. "I will not leave you as orphans; I will come to you," He assured both His disciples and us (John 14:18).

Have you set your eyes on someone or something other than the Everlasting Father this Christmas? If so, remember that, even now, Jesus is reaching out to take your hand and to reassure you that all is well.

Just what any good father would do.

E.Y.

NINE

THE JOURNAL

The LORD disciplines those he loves,
as a father the son he delights in.

*I*t had been a long time since Mark Garfield had seen the old place: 1724 Johnson Street, Rosston, Illinois. Nearly thirty years had passed since he'd lived there and more than twenty since he'd laid eyes on it.

In some ways, it looked the same: rosebushes out front; small, detached garage behind; hedge along the south side of the property. And yet the years had clearly taken a toll. Brittle, green paint peeled off in great patches, revealing weathered wood siding in desperate need of repair. The hedge, neatly trimmed in memory, now grew wildly in an unruly tangle. Gone was the trellis by the front door that once provided a beautiful and tidy home for the fragrant red roses that grew there every spring. And one other thing caught Mark's attention: the battered FOR SALE sign planted unceremoniously in the front yard.

Mark sighed as he tried to reconcile old memories with current reality. It hadn't been his idea to make this pilgrimage to the town where he had grown up. It had been a good year for his consulting business, and he wanted to do something special for his ten-year-old son, Scott, whom he rightly suspected felt neglected in the torrent of Mark's hectic work schedule.

"Scott," Mark had said one day early that fall, "how would you like it if you and I took a trip somewhere special—just the two of us? Mom and Lauren will stay home. This'll be just a guy thing. What do you think?"

Scott's eyes grew big, and his mouth fell open. He searched his father's face, looking for some sign that this was just another of Dad's little "jokes." But Mark just smiled.

"You *mean* it?" Scott asked. "*Really?* Dad, if you're for real, I'd love it!" Scott wrapped his little arms around his father's waist, burying his head in his torso, and then looked up.

"Where are we going?" he asked. "And when?"

Mark laughed. "That's the best part," he replied. "*You* get to choose the place. So long as it's within reason, you can name anywhere in the country you'd like to visit. Disneyland. The Smithsonian. Dinosaur National Monument. The

Kennedy Space Center. You pick the place, and so long as we can do the whole trip in five days, that's where we go. I'm taking off the first week in December, and you can consider this sort of a pre-Christmas gift. So—what's your pleasure?"

Scott gave his dad another tight squeeze and then released his grip. He pulled away and locked his hands behind his head, as he did whenever he started to think deeply about something. For several minutes he paced excitedly in a ragged little circle.

Mark chuckled again, delighted to see his son's bright, young mind off and running. He knew Scott well enough to know that his boy would probably want time to think about his choice; no impulsive child, this. But Mark also strongly suspected that, in the end, Scott would choose a place that challenged his mind—a science museum, a wildlife refuge, perhaps even a dinosaur dig. After all, this was the kid who, for two years running, had chosen to trick-or-treat as a paleontologist. Mark knew his son well, and that's why Scott's choice completely surprised him.

"Dad," he said slowly, "I think I know where I'd like to go."

"So soon?" asked Mark, startled. "I thought you'd want to take some time to think about it."

"Usually I would," Scott answered, "but lately I've been wondering about something. Dad, I'd like to go to Chicago.

We could visit both the Museum of Science and Industry and the Field Museum—and we could also take a day or two to visit where you grew up. I'd like to see Rosston, Dad."

Rosston? It never occurred to Scott that his son might want to see Rosston. Why would anyone want to visit that decaying, dying little burg? Scott had fled town as soon as he graduated from high school, and since his parents had moved out of town shortly afterward, he had never returned.

"Why…would you want to see Rosston?" Mark asked. "Wouldn't you rather spend our time someplace *fun?* Remember, in early December it could be really cold in northern Illinois. Wouldn't you rather visit someplace warm, maybe in Florida or out West?"

Scott shook his head. "Dad," he said, "you said *I* could choose. And I'd like to see Rosston. You hardly ever talk about it, I've never seen any pictures, and I'd like to see where you grew up. Grandma and Grandpa died when I was really little, and I don't remember them very well. In school we've been studying family histories, and I don't know much about yours. So can't we go to Rosston?"

So that's how Mark and Scott Garfield wound up in a rental car on a brisk, gray December day, staring from the curb at 1724 Johnson Street. They had arrived in town the previous day and stayed that night at the old Driftwood Motel, a relic even during Mark's boyhood days. A drive by the old family homestead revealed the FOR SALE sign, and Mark called the realtor to arrange a visit. He learned the house had been on the market, off and on, for more than two years—yet another victim of a dying community. When manufacturing jobs started going overseas a decade or more before, the population began to decline, and now a number of homes went unsold for lack of buyers. Count 1724 Johnson as just another fading ghost haunting the old neighborhood.

When the Realtor pulled up in an aging '84 El Dorado, the Garfields got out to greet her. She shook hands, made a beeline for a lockbox attached to the bottom of the porch railing, extracted a house key, and invited father and son to enter.

"If you don't mind, I'll let you conduct your own tour," she said pleasantly to Mark. "After all, you no doubt know the place better than I do. I have some business I need to take care of, so I'll be in my car if you need me for anything. Happy memories!"

She turned, closed the door behind her, and left Mark and Scott to explore on their own. Mark stood in the hallway for a moment as if to retrieve a mental blueprint of his old stomping grounds.

"Well, this is it," he sighed. "There's really not much to the tour. This house is small by today's standards: the living room to your left, the kitchen straight ahead, and three bedrooms through the kitchen and to the left. The basement is down that door to the right, but I don't expect there's much to see. My dad never finished it, and most folks around here use their basements for storage."

Scott did a quick reconnaissance and then said, "Dad, could I see your room?"

Mark nodded, set off through the kitchen, ambled down a narrow hallway, and stopped by the last door on the left. "My brother and I shared this room," he said as he peered through the doorway. He flipped a light switch, and a small room with a battered wooden floor leapt into view. Scott slid past his dad into the center of the room, floorboards creaking all the way. He soon spotted some childish drawings on the corner wall, down by the floor. He pointed to them.

"Did you do that, Dad?"

Mark looked and shook his head. "No, Son, that looks to be the work of someone who lived here after I left." But even as he spoke, his eye traveled from the drawing to a spot about a foot away. There he saw another young artist's rendering that he did recognize. He drew near, bent down, reached out a finger, and remembered.

He laughed. "Scott, come here," he said. "You see this carving in the baseboard? You wouldn't know it, but it's supposed to be a picture of Ron Santo."

"Ron Santo?" Scott asked. "Who's he?"

"He used to play for the Cubs," Mark replied, "and I

wanted to play with him someday. But when my dad found out what I did to his baseboard, I didn't think I'd *ever* play baseball again, whether with Ron Santo or with Ricky next door. Man, was he mad!"

As Mark inspected his work, the old carving triggered another memory buried long ago. Immediately he rose, turned, and strode over to the closet. "I wonder…" he murmured. He opened the closet door, got down on his knees, and fiddled with a loose board at the back of the closet.

"What are you doing?" Scott asked, but Mark didn't hear the question. Moments later he emerged from the closet, grinning and holding what appeared to be two old books.

"Come over here and sit next to me, Son," Mark said softly as he turned the books over in his hands. "I can't believe these are still here after all these years."

"What *are* they, Dad?" Scott asked. His paleontological imagination had been stirred, and he clambered for a closer look.

Mark untied an old string that bound the two volumes together and began to explain. "That carving got me into a lot of trouble," he said. "I'm lucky my dad had become a Christian a few years before. Otherwise I think he would have thrashed me good. I was about your age, maybe a little younger, and I knew better. I got grounded *and* a spanking, of course, but my dad felt like I needed something more. I think my mom had something to do with my final punishment." He paused, and his son, eager for a little family history, urged him on.

"What happened?" wondered Scott.

"*This* happened," Mark replied, holding up the two books. "My dad was smart but never got to finish school. He had to go to work to take care of his family, and although he could read, he couldn't do it very well. I, on the other hand, loved to read, and he gave me an assignment that I couldn't refuse, if you know what I mean."

Scott grinned and nodded.

"He knew I resented the spanking, but he also knew I had become a Christian shortly before he did. So he gave me a blank book, a journal—this one right here—and a Bible, and told me to look for all the verses I could find about 'chastening'—what we'd call 'discipline.' When I found one, I was supposed to write it in my journal, along with what I thought the verse was teaching."

"But why was it still in the closet?" asked Scott. "Why didn't you or your dad keep it?"

Mark ruffled his son's brown hair and replied, "To tell the truth, I didn't much care for the assignment. Oh, I did the work, but I didn't want my dad to see what I had written. I kept the journal and my Bible in that secret compartment in the closet so he wouldn't read what I wrote. And then we lost the house."

Scott shot his dad a puzzled look. "What do you mean, you 'lost the house?' How could you lose it when it's still here?"

"It's a long story, Son," Mark replied sadly, "but basically, we had to move. The factory where Dad worked closed down, and the only job he could find for quite a while was delivering pizzas. In the chaos of moving, I forgot about the books, and when Dad asked me about them later, I lied and said I must have lost them in the move. They've stayed here ever since."

Father and son said nothing for some time. Then finally Scott asked, "Well…can we *read* them?"

"I don't see why not," Mark replied.

Mark opened his journal to the first page, written in a child's unsteady scrawl. Together they read the following words: *2 Samuel 7:14 — "I will be his father, and he shall be my son. If he commit iniquity, I will chasten him with the rod of men, and with the stripes of the children of men."*

Next to the Bible text, in red pencil, a chastened Mark Garfield had written: *God says He will chasten King David's son with a rod when he sins. BUT HE DOESN'T SAY NOTHING ABOUT GROUNDING HIM.*

They both laughed and kept reading. Further down the page, they found another interesting entry: *Proverbs 19:18—* *"Chasten thy son while there is hope, and let not thy soul spare for his crying."*

They noted the commentary, again in red pencil: *God tells fathers to chasten their sons before they do anything really bad, and He says they shouldn't stop just because the kid cries. OK, maybe I deserved a spanking, but Jimmy Miller does a lot worse than me, and he NEVER gets a whipping. That's not fair.*

For the next twenty minutes or so, father and son sat on the floor of Mark's boyhood bedroom and eagerly read the pages of his secret "discipline journal." Mark soon noted a trend: The more his young self studied God's wisdom on the issue of discipline, the less put out the boy felt. He especially marveled at his youthful comments on Hebrews 12:5-6,11: *"My son, despise not thou the chastening of the Lord, nor faint when thou art rebuked of him: For whom the Lord loveth he chasteneth, and scourgeth every son whom he receiveth.... Now no chastening for the present seemeth to be joyous, but grievous; nevertheless afterward it yieldeth the peaceable fruit of right-eousness..."*

In red pencil, a disciplined Mark Garfield had written: *God, I'm sorry for getting mad at my dad. It's easy to forget he punishes me because he loves me. Jimmy Miller told me today that he wished he had a dad who loved him enough to give him a whipping, and when I tried to tell him he was nuts, he punched me in the arm and ran away. I used to wish I was Jimmy Miller. Not anymore.*

By the time they reached the final entry, Mark Garfield was in tears, and Scott Garfield was grinning ear to ear. Next to Revelation 3:19—*"As many as I love, I rebuke and chasten: be zealous therefore, and repent"*—they saw that a maturing young man had written: *Here it is again. Jesus says that He rebukes and chastens everyone He loves. He doesn't punish people because He's mad, but because He loves them. I know how my dad punishes me. But how does Jesus chasten and rebuke us? What does He do?*

And there the journal ended, untouched and unread for almost thirty years.

"Dad?" Scott said.

"Yes, Son?" Mark replied.

"Dad, do you think we could take these books home with us?"

"I'll ask the Realtor, but I doubt she'll mind. They don't add anything to the value of the home."

"I think you're wrong there, Dad," Scott replied. "I think they add a lot to the value of *our* home. Thanks for bringing me to Rosston." With that, he wrapped his father in a big bear hug.

"Thanks for insisting on it," Mark answered. "But you know, there's a price to pay."

Scott cocked his head, drew apart, and slowly said, "Um…what do you mean?"

"I see that I never really finished my assignment," Mark replied. "I think I need to. And I'd like to ask for your help. Do you think we could find the time to talk about this together? I left a pretty big question hanging in my journal."

"You bet, Dad!" cried Scott, wrapping his dad in another monster hug.

You know, Mark thought, *this isn't a bad way to begin Christmas. And maybe Rosston's not so terrible after all.*

S.H.

TEN

A Cure for
Troubled Hearts

Let not your heart be troubled.

JOHN 14:1 (NASB)

*I*t was a night to remember. Eleven men reclined at the
table after finishing the Passover meal, listening intently
to their Everlasting Father. They didn't know it, but Jesus was
about to give them His farewell address.

"My children," He said, "I will be with you only a little
longer. You will look for me, and just as I told the Jews, so I
tell you now: Where I am going, you cannot come" (John
13:33). In just twenty-four hours, Jesus would bring human

history to its climax: He would make atonement for the sins of humanity.

The unexpected news of His imminent departure greatly troubled the disciples, however. These men had left their families to follow Him. They had quit their jobs. After landing the catch of a lifetime, Simon and Andrew and their companions, James and John, left their boats and fish-filled nets to follow Him. Matthew abandoned his post at the tax office. They all had left the hopes and dreams of their careers to follow Him.

And Jesus had become a father to them. He taught them about the kingdom of God. He provided for their physical and emotional needs. He healed Peter's mother-in-law (Matthew 8:14-15). He gave away five loaves of bread and two fish to feed the multitude, yet still had enough for the disciples (Mark 6:38-43). He defended His disciples against the Pharisees (Matthew 12:1-8). He listened to their questions. He corrected their errors. He spent time with them in public and in private. Jesus loved these men. Can you imagine how they reacted to the news that He would soon be leaving them?

Jesus was aware of their troubled hearts. He knew of their fears and uncertainties. He knew that in a few days they would stand before the cross in grief and mourning. He sensed their fears. And like a wise father, He comforted them.

The Way It "Ought to Be"

In a way that can surprise us, Christmas can be one of the most troubling times of the year. Our culture exalts Christmas and treasures its traditions, so most of us have a fairly distinct sense of how Christmas "ought to be." We think Christmas means being surrounded by family members whom we love and who love us. In countless commercials, television shows, songs, books, and magazine ads, we see Christmas the way it "ought to be."

But if your life situation does not live up to this mythical ideal, Christmas can be a time of terrible loneliness and alienation. Perhaps this is your first Christmas without a loved one. Maybe your friends are now married and rearing families, while you're still single. It used to be okay—you still got included—but as the years have sped by, your singleness seems increasingly out of place.

Besides all of that, we live in a troubled world twelve months of the year. We live in a place and time that supply ample heartache for everybody. Some of us feel like the man in a Noel Coward play who was trying to run away from life. When someone asked him, "Why are you running away?" he answered, "The past depresses me. The future confuses me. And the present scares me to death." We want to run because our hearts are troubled.

Amid all this confusion, the Everlasting Father steps into our lives and says to us, "Do not let your hearts be troubled" (John 14:1). The comfort of our Everlasting Father surpasses that of anyone else—even that of the best earthly father—for His comfort originates from the endless reservoirs of His divine grace and mercy. His comfort brings a soul-settling peace sufficient for all our uncertainties and all our sorrows. And His comfort is everlasting because He is everlasting.

COMFORT IN TRUST

Jesus did not stop after saying, "Do not let your hearts be troubled." He also gave His disciples free access to several powerful resources, each of which can bring great comfort. The first is this: "Trust in God; trust also in me" (John 14:1).

What does it mean to trust in God or to trust in Christ? In essence, it means to place your whole confidence in the Lord's ability to keep His promises and to take care of you, regardless of how grim things may look. One popular definition declares that "faith is believing in advance what will make sense only in reverse." When we really trust someone—when that someone has earned our total confidence—we follow that person's instruction whether it seems to make sense to us or not.

One day when I was about fifteen years old, my dad came home from work to find a pecan tree that he had ordered from a mail-order company. Immediately he wanted to plant the tree in our backyard even though the sky was spitting rain.

"Come on, Edwin," he said, "we're going to plant that tree."

I followed my dad outside, and I have to tell you that the tree looked as if it had roots five feet long. I've never *seen* such roots.

"Start digging," my dad said. And man, I began to dig in that Mississippi mud. I dug, and I dug, and I dug, and I dug—I thought I'd never get deep enough.

"Can't we just kind of force those roots?" I pleaded.

"No, you've got to get them all the way down," Dad replied.

So I dug and I dug some more. Finally we planted that pecan tree. By that time I was tired, wet, and angry.

"When are we going to have some pecans?" I demanded.

Dad answered, "I'll probably not live long enough to ever harvest that tree."

I stormed into the house thinking, *That's about the dumbest thing I've ever been a part of.*

But the last time I drove by our old house—someone else lives there now—I glanced into the backyard. And there, right where I had dug and dug and dug years ago, was the biggest pecan tree you'd ever want to see. *Somebody's* harvesting those pecans today. My dad knew what he was doing after all, even though his plan made no sense to me. His vision was bigger than mine and his experience greater. Imagine how much more I would have enjoyed that moment so long ago had I trusted my dad.

There's wonderful comfort to be found when we place our trust in the Everlasting Father. He knows the end from the beginning and He does everything well. Are you struggling with one or more of His commands that seem to make no sense? Are you confused about some of the things He has allowed to happen to you or your loved ones? Or does the clamor of the season have you tied up in knots? If you want the comfort available from the Savior, you must place your full trust in Him. He's promised to take care of you, and He will do so faithfully regardless of whether His plan seems to make sense at the time.

COMFORT IN THE FATHER'S HOUSE

Jesus gave His disciples a second dose of comfort. "In my Father's house are many rooms," He said; "if it were not so, I would have told you. I am going there to prepare a place for you" (John 14:2).

As Christians, we have the tremendous comfort of a future and final destination called heaven, the dwelling place of

God is omnipresent, of course, but in a special way He abides in heaven where His will and His way rule supremely.

Jesus calls heaven His "Father's house" and describes it as a splendid place with many rooms. This heavenly home is not the Holy Hotel. You don't have to worry about getting stuck on the thousandth floor when all the activity is taking place in the downstairs lounge. Neither do you need to feel anxious about getting lost in the crowd. Rather, the Father's house is a residence. Heaven will be a true home for all of us.

Our Everlasting Father has plenty of room in heaven, space set aside for you and for me. Each occupant will receive individualized attention. The Good Shepherd calls His own sheep by name and will have a special place prepared for each of His lambs. He will have a crown to fit you that no one else can wear and a dwelling place just for you.

Like a wise father who provides his sons and daughters with a safe home—a place of refuge and healing—Jesus Christ provides for us an eternal place where we will find comfort and peace.

Heaven brings comfort to us today by assuring us that the pain and suffering we endure on this earth is temporary. We also find comfort in knowing that those in Christ who have gone before us are now in the Father's house, and we find peace in knowing that we will see them again. And even now, in a unique way, we can experience the comfort of heaven here on earth as we grow in our relationship with the Everlasting Father.

COMFORT IN A PROMISE

Since Jesus, like His Father, is "the Father of compassion and the God of all comfort" (2 Corinthians 1:3), He keeps finding ways to comfort His children. The disciples found this to be true in a special promise of Jesus. The Lord told them, "I will do whatever you ask in my name, so that the Son may bring glory to the Father. You may ask me for anything in my name, and I will do it" (John 14:13-14).

What a statement! Here the Everlasting Father opens a door for all those with troubled hearts. We are welcome, anytime, to approach Him with our needs and our troubles. Think of it: Jesus is waiting to give *you* comfort this Christmas! All that is required is that you ask and that your request be consistent with His good and perfect will. When we pray along these lines, He grants us our request because we ask in the name and for the glory of Jesus.

This is an unqualified promise, a blank check. Ask anything you want—in His name and for His glory. Is it any wonder that our troubled hearts can find comfort in Jesus' astonishing promises?

Do you remember sitting on Santa's lap as a child? I

recall the excitement and the anticipation of telling Santa all my Christmas needs and wants. (I had lots of both!) While he made a list and checked it twice to see if I'd been naughty or nice, *I* was making a list of all my wants and desires and checking it twice. I was ready to let him have it!

Our Everlasting Father, with much greater wisdom, sits and waits for us to crawl into the comfort of His lap to express our needs. He wants our wish list…and He delivers!

What's on your Christmas list this season? I recommend that you make a list of all the relationships and situations in your life to which God wants to bring peace and comfort. He is ready and willing; all you need to do is ask.

COMFORT IN A HELPER

The disciples found great comfort in Christ's person and promise. They found additional comfort in the hope of their future residence. But what about the meantime? How were they to live? How were they to enjoy the comfort and security of their Lord and Savior in His absence?

Many of us have thought, *Boy, it would be great if Jesus came and lived among us today. Christianity would be so much easier.* When we had a question for Him, we could just send Him an e-mail. If our child or loved one was sick, He could just come over and heal them.

While the time has not yet arrived for Christ's return, the Everlasting Father has anticipated the needs of His children. He knew we would need embraces and encouraging words on this side of heaven. He knew the disciples' need for help (ours, too!), and He knew our need for comfort. So He sent a Helper called the Holy Spirit.

For example, a mother and her son attended church every week. One Sunday morning the mother felt too sick to attend, so she said to her son, "You go on to church without me." The boy went to church, and when he returned home, his mom asked, "Son, what did the preacher talk about this morning?"

"I can't remember," he replied.

"Did you *go* to church?" she asked.

"Oh yes!"

"Then you must know what the preacher preached about. Tell me."

The young man thought for a moment and then answered, "Oh yeah. I got it! He preached about...uh... uh...'Don't worry, you'll get the blanket.'"

Don't worry, you'll get the blanket? his mother wondered.

She had no idea what her son meant, so the following Sunday as she was leaving the worship service she asked the preacher, "Pastor, by the way, what did you preach on last Sunday?"

The minister replied, "I called my sermon, 'Fear Not, I'll Send You the Comforter.'"

None of us has to fear being left all alone, for Jesus told His disciples, "And I will ask the Father, and He will give you another Helper, that He may be with you forever.... He will teach you all things, and bring to your remembrance all that I said to you. Peace I leave with you; My peace I give to you; not as the world gives, do I give to you. Let not your heart be troubled, nor let it be fearful" (John 14:16,26-27, NASB).

God has sent His Comforter, His Helper—the Holy Spirit. The word used in the original Greek for "counselor" or "comforter" means "one who comes alongside of." The Holy Spirit comes alongside and helps us with that broken relationship, that lost loved one, or that impossible situation. And He comes alongside us at the point where our burdens weigh us down the most and says, "I'll give you the strength to carry on."

Charles Schultz, the late creator of the *Peanuts* cartoon strip, understood well our need for comfort. He created Linus, knowing that we would all identify with this boy's need for comfort and security.

Do you feel like Linus without his blanket this Christmas season? When sorrow and pain envelop us, many of us crawl underneath our favorite blanket. With that blanket, we wipe our tears and hide from the world. We shut down and sleep to try to remedy our pain and emptiness.

While the Holy Spirit doesn't encourage us to pretend that things are different from what they really are, He does bring us the perfect "blanket," the comfort of the Everlasting Father Himself.

THE PEACE OF THE LORD

Just a few weeks before Christmas, Johnny sat at the kitchen table making his wish list. He wrote down a few items, paused for a moment, and then wrote some more. His mother passed by and saw his long list.

"Oh my, Johnny!" she exclaimed. "We can't afford all of these things! If you could pick just one thing for Christmas, what would it be?"

The little boy paused for a long moment, looked at the picture of his absent father hanging on the wall, and said to his mom, "I wish Dad would step out of that picture."

The wish of that little boy has been the wish of all thoughtful men and women since the beginning of the world: "I wish the Father, God, would step out of eternity and enter time." And yet it remained largely a wish...until Christmas!

John writes, "The Word became flesh, and dwelt among

us" (John 1:14, NASB). That is Christmas! God became visible and touchable in the person of Jesus Christ.

Like a dear father, Jesus continues to bring us unending comfort. This Christmas, take some time to break away from the busyness of the season. And in the silence of your own reflection, enjoy the peace and comfort that come only from abiding in the Everlasting Father.

E.Y.

ELEVEN

A PRODIGAL CHRISTMAS

"For this son of mine was dead and is alive again; he was lost and is found." So they began to celebrate.

Christmas incarnates all five senses.

We can *see* Christmas. We see both the lights adorning the homes and businesses of small towns and the lights shining in a pattern from within the city's tall buildings. We can *smell* Christmas. How delightful to smell the tree, the freshly cut holly, or the sweet aroma of a favorite dish drifting in from the kitchen. And then we can *taste* Christmas—the turkey, dressing, pies, cookies, and eggnog. We also *hear* Christmas on our radios and in the department stores. And at what other time of the year can we hear the ringing of the Salvation Army bell? We can also *touch* Christmas—the bristle of the Christmas pines, the ripping of wrapping paper, and the embrace of loved ones.

With all of this, how could anyone miss Christmas? Even those who reject Christianity sing "Silent Night" when the lights go out and the candles are lit. With all the sights and sounds and smells and tastes and feel of Christmas, how do we miss it?

We miss it when we leave the Baby in the manger.

A BABY MAKES NO DEMANDS

Who can resist a little baby? I don't believe I have ever seen a baby who wasn't cute. A few barely make it, but they still qualify. Babies are warm, loving, cuddly, and fun. And when we see a baby in a manger, we aren't threatened. Such a baby has no authority over us. He does not make demands or require anything from us.

But that little Baby left the manger and "grew in wisdom and stature, and in favor with God and men" (Luke 2:52). The Infant matured and became the Everlasting Father to many of us. He became a Man who faced the trials and temptations that we, too, experience.

It's the full-grown Jesus who says to you and to me, "Change your way. Repent. And come, follow Me." This grown Babe is the Jesus many of us don't want to face, so we leave Him "away in a manger" in that sweet, little-boy state. When we leave the Baby in the manger, however, we miss the enormous impact He desires to make on our hearts. We miss the most important part of what Christmas is all about.

THE FATHER OF FORGIVENESS

Jesus Christ is our Everlasting Father in many ways, not the least of which is His status as the Father of our faith. Scripture calls Him the Author of Life (Acts 3:15), the Author of Our Salvation (Hebrews 2:10), and the Author and Perfecter of Our Faith (Hebrews 12:2). As God incarnate, He is the Mediator between God and us (1 Timothy 2:5), and so became the Founder of Our Salvation. In this sense, Jesus Christ is the Father of Forgiveness.

He made this clear when He spoke to His disciples: "Thus it is written, that the Christ should suffer and rise again from the dead the third day; and that repentance for the forgiveness of sins should be proclaimed in His name to all the nations, beginning from Jerusalem" (Luke 24:46-47, NASB).

Now, two thousand years later, we are receiving the everlasting pardon that He promised so long ago. He signed and sealed our forgiveness at the Cross. We *receive* His forgiveness when we turn from our sins and trust in Him alone for our salvation. We *experience* His forgiveness on a daily basis through the confession of sin.

Our Everlasting Father could not teach us by His own moral mistakes, for He made none. He modeled perfect relationships with His Father in heaven and with those around Him. He modeled unconditional forgiveness by dying on a cross to make atonement for our sins. He came that we might find forgiveness and reconciliation with God and with others.

He Recognizes Us from Afar

This Christmas season, if we are looking for a picture of what forgiveness does and how it works, we could do no better than to consider the story of the prodigal son (Luke 15:11-27). This young man's story vividly demonstrates that our heavenly Father's forgiveness is free, unconditional, and everlasting.

The foolish youth left home, squandered the inheritance from his father, and hit bottom. Out of both money and options, he was forced to feed pigs in a pigpen, hoping that he might get to eat some tiny morsel of their food. Perhaps in a puddle of water that somehow remained uncontaminated by the mud, the filth, and the stench, the prodigal saw a reflection of himself. He blinked his eyes and looked again, but he barely recognized the haggard face looking back at him from the water. *Who is that?* he wondered. *I don't know that man. I've never seen him before!*

Suddenly the man realized what a pitiful figure he had become. Then, in Jesus' dramatic words, "He came to himself." It was a turning point. The life of the prodigal changed in a moment, and he determined to go home.

When the prodigal had first left home, he said, "I want." In the pigpen, he became a person "in want." But when he returned home, he discovered that *his father wanted him!* All the time, the father had wanted him. The prodigal didn't know it, nor did he understand it. But as soon as his father saw his boy, he had compassion on him and ran to embrace and kiss his returning son.

How could the father have recognized his son? Long, hard years had passed. The young man probably had a scraggly beard by then. His tattered clothes lay loosely over his emaciated frame. Dissipation, degradation, and hard labor had aged him beyond his years. But even from far away, the father recognized him. How did he manage it? He recognized him by his walk—that's the key to recognizing a person from a distance.

You may feel as though you've wandered a long way from your heavenly Father. You may have been gone for years, and perhaps your appearance has changed dramatically. You don't look the same as you did in younger, happier days. Do you long to return home, but worry that your Father won't recognize you after all the hard miles that have weathered your tired, old body?

Worry no longer. The Everlasting Father recognizes you all right. He remembers how you move, and although your gait may have slowed to a shuffle, He knows you all the same. And He wants to welcome you home with a joyful, loving embrace.

He Runs to Us

The most revolutionary, startling thing in the story of the prodigal son is its picture of a father running to meet his boy. Nowhere else in the Bible do we see God running.

Many Jewish scholars who have read this story contend that this is beyond belief. The Talmud teaches that a man of affluence and prestige should never run in public. Aristotle said, "Great men never run in public." In the Eastern world it is unthinkable for a father to forget his dignity, his position, and his age by picking up his robe and running to meet his boy.

Yet that's exactly what the father did in Jesus' story.

This parable teaches us that, when God sees one of His wayward children start back home to Him, He doesn't care a fig about dignity or pride or what anyone else might think. He just runs to meet the child who's coming home!

Isn't it thrilling to know that God loves us and wants us close to Him? He underscores this wonderful news every Christmas by reminding us that our Lord ran the distance from heaven to earth to be born into the human family. He hurdled the obstacles of natural laws and physics to be born of a virgin mother. Why? Only one reason: to embrace us and secure us in the everlasting arms of His forgiveness.

He Demonstrates His Forgiveness

Notice something else from this story about the Everlasting Father: When He forgives, He gives. Giving follows His forgiving.

We humans often do the opposite. Even if we forgive someone, we tend to put that individual on probation. We let him linger in purgatory for a while, withholding a little love and a little responsibility until our hurts diminish and he demonstrates that he has changed his ways. Only then do we restore the full rights and privileges of a close friendship.

But Jesus operates differently. When He forgives, He gives—demonstrating the sufficiency and permanence of His forgiveness. The father in Jesus' story said, "Bring the best robe and put it on him." This was a festival robe, the first mark that the returning son was still part of the family. The father then said, "Put a ring on his finger, and sandals on his feet." The ring was probably a signet ring, which gave the young man power of attorney. Giving him that ring was like giving back the rascal's credit cards. Remember, this is the same boy who shamed his father by taking his inheritance and wasting it on the stuff of the world. After all those years in a distant country, he came back depleted, his pathetic life nothing but a tale of debauchery. And yet the father immediately said, "Come home. Take the robe; wear the ring. I'm giving back your VISA and MasterCard. I'm restoring you to the position you once enjoyed."

At best, the prodigal had hoped that his father would take him in as a *mishtash* servant, the lowest kind of slave. *Mishtash* servants worked and served barefooted. They could not own or afford shoes; having shoes meant you were a part of the family. The son could not hope for that; he felt utterly desperate and broken. Yet his father gave him the best robe, the family ring, and the finest sandals—and the son knew that he was home.

The celebration began immediately. The father called for a fattened calf to be slaughtered for the homecoming feast. Now think about that for a moment. What brought the prodigal home? What preacher caused the prodigal to get up out of the pigpen? Hunger!

Empty stomachs have preached some of the most eloquent sermons in history. When the boy's stomach started growling, he came to himself and turned toward home. We can only imagine his hunger as he entered the front gate of his father's estate. When he left the pigs, he had enormous needs. He was in great want. And then he made that great discovery—the greatest discovery anybody can ever make. He discovered that he was *wanted*. The father wanted him home and offered him complete forgiveness, no questions asked.

As we celebrate His season, perhaps you need to find forgiveness from the Everlasting Father. If so, ask Him today to forgive you. And know that regardless of your sin, regardless of what you have done or how far and how long you've been away, the Everlasting Father still loves you. He still cares for you. He wants to embrace you in His loving arms, to restore you to His family, to clothe and shower you with His true riches. He waits, anxiously looking for your familiar walk— the weakened, humbled walk of His wandering son or daughter heading home at last.

COME HOME

Years ago, my friend Jess Moody served as pastor of the First Baptist Church in West Palm Beach, Florida. At that time,

Jimmy Carter was running for president, and everybody seemed to be talking about being "born again."

One evening Dr. Moody was sitting on the platform at a $1,000-a-plate benefit dinner for special-needs children. Seated next to him was the keynote speaker, Mrs. Rose Kennedy, the mother of John F. Kennedy. During a pleasant conversation, she looked over to the Baptist preacher and said, "Dr. Moody, you might be interested to know that I am a born-again Christian."

"Mrs. Kennedy, tell me about it," Dr. Moody replied.

"Well," she said, "when Joe and I were first married, our wedding was the social event of the year. I was a New York debutante, and he was from a well-known family in Massachusetts. Our wedding got a big write-up in the *New York Times*. Many VIPs came as our special guests. It was a thrilling moment.

"Our first year of marriage was just heaven on earth. He couldn't love me enough; I couldn't love him enough. A few years later, our first son, Joe Jr., was born. He was just the apple of his daddy's eye."

But things were soon to change.

"Then our second child was born deformed, retarded," she continued. "Joe did not know how to handle it. He turned on me and blamed me for the child's problems. He blamed me for the shame and embarrassment he felt. Suddenly, where we had been close, we began to move in different directions. He went off in his own world, and I began to drink too much."

Mrs. Kennedy paused and then looked Dr. Moody in the eye. "Pastor," she said, "one afternoon one of my maids had not done something I had asked her to do. I turned to her and began to lambaste her and castigate her. At the end of my words of rebuke, I said, 'You make me so unhappy.'"

The maid turned and looked at her employer and very graciously said, "Mrs. Kennedy, until you make out of your heart a manger for Jesus to be born, you'll never be happy."

That did it. In a rage, Mrs. Kennedy fired the maid on the spot. But later that night something unexpected happened.

"At about a quarter to three in the morning," she explained, "I was awakened. Suddenly all of my life flashed before me, and I saw every sin of commission and every sin of omission of which I was guilty. I began to cry. I got down and bent my Roman Catholic knees and cried out to God: 'O God, make out of my heart a manger for Jesus to be born!' At that moment, I invited Jesus Christ to come into my life, and I became a born-again Christian."

Rose Kennedy lived to the ripe old age of 105. She died

on January 22, 1995, and many in the press marveled at her ability to handle everything that life had thrown at her. For many years her husband had openly kept many mistresses and trained his sons to do the same. Her oldest child, Joe Jr., had died in World War II. Her son John, the president of the United States, died from an assassin's bullet. A younger son Robert died a few years later while running for president, the victim of another assassin's bullet. The tragedies striking her family just did not seem to stop.

Yet because Rose Kennedy sought forgiveness from the Everlasting Father, she weathered every hardship throughout her 105 eventful years.

The same can be true for you.

This Christmas, make out of *your* heart a manger for Jesus to be born. Come home to the Everlasting Father and receive His freely offered forgiveness.

E.Y.

TWELVE

NATIVITY LEMONS

I have set you an example that you should do as I have done for you.

JOHN 13:15

Lemonade! I need another lemonade!"

Lyn Hafziger turned frantically to her stage manager, her tired eyes full of desperation. The annual Christmas play at Sonrise Community Church refused to move in a happy direction, and Lyn didn't know what to do. She quickly glanced at Pastor Barnes, who stood watching from a corner. Four weeks ago he had told Lyn that the church lacked good actors, and right now she deeply regretted her glib reply: "Well, when you've got lemons, make lemonade!"

Now she was drinking her words.

Yet Lyn refused to give up. She had promised the pastor that she would try to bring a little professionalism to the holiday production, and she planned to stick to her promise even if it killed her. And it might. *What I wouldn't give to be the real John the Baptist right now,* she thought as, onstage, Jimmy Kerrings once more violently popped a packet of ketchup on his neck—despite explicit direction—to simulate the Baptist's demise.

"Jimmy, please, we've discussed this," Lyn called out. "I know you think it adds to the drama of the scene, but it's too much of a distraction. We need to let the narrator handle that part. Okay? Please? Now I need you to go wash off."

Jimmy shrugged, thrust his hands in his pockets (to make sure he still had an ample supply of ketchup), and walked offstage to the bathroom. Lyn had no way of knowing it, but she already *had* brought more professionalism to the church play than it had ever enjoyed. Yet no one could miss her look of dismay, and Pastor Barnes took advantage of the unscheduled break to offer some welcome news.

"Lyn," he said, "may I interrupt?"

Lyn turned and replied meekly, "Pastor, I *promise* we'll get the ketchup stain off the carpet. We really aren't going to chop John's head off onstage and—"

Pastor Barnes cut her off with a chuckle. "Hey, Lyn, I haven't come to offer ministerial direction. From what I can see, you've already taken us further than we've ever been. No, I came to let you know that I might have a line on a fellow to play Jesus in the play…and he's *good.*"

Lyn fell into a chair, surprised. Pastor Barnes strode out from the shadows and took a seat next to her.

"Try not to look so apoplectic," he laughed. "Lyn, you've done a great job with what you have, but I know you've struggled to find a decent Jesus." The pastor checked himself, cocked his head, and said, "Can I *say* that? Anyway, I think I may have found him."

The news seemed impossibly good to Lyn. She always believed she could get a handle on the ketchup-wielding Jimmys and the melodramatic Nancys, but so far she had failed to come up with a passable Jesus—and the whole play depended upon him. For this year the church board decided it wanted not just another Nativity play, but a production that showed how Christmas set the stage for Easter. It wanted an original performance that began with the birth of Jesus and ended with the resurrected Christ.

"Lyn," Pastor Barnes continued, "I just got off the phone with a fellow named Rick Watson. He's new to the area and has visited Sonrise the last couple of weeks. He told me that for many years he's been active in community theater and even did several television commercials in the Sacramento area. He and his wife are baby Christians—they both accepted the Lord about a month ago—and when his employer transferred him out here, the man who led him to Christ strongly urged him to get involved in a local church.

They like Sonrise, and he wanted to know if there is still time to help out with the Christmas play. Isn't that *great?*"

Lyn gulped. "Oh, Pastor," she answered, "it sounds like an answer to prayer!" She meant *desperate, begging, weeping, sackcloth-and-ashes* prayer, but she didn't say so. But then a nasty thought chilled her blood, and she grabbed the pastor's arm. "You…you told him we'd *love* to have him, didn't you?" she pleaded.

Pastor Barnes patted her hand and said reassuringly, "I certainly did. I asked for his number and told him you'd be calling. Here it is." He held out a note with a scrawled phone number. Lyn snatched the precious paper from her pastor's hand and thought, for just a moment, that she heard an angelic choir singing the "Hallelujah Chorus."

Thank You, Lord! she exulted.

Lyn could hardly wait for the next practice. She faxed Rick the working script for the play and, at the rehearsal, discovered to her delight that he already had his part nearly memorized. With great anticipation she watched as the wedding supper at Cana began to unfold. Rick had a tremendous stage presence, and the actors around him fed off of it. A thrill shot through Lyn as she watched a *real* actor perform under her direction.

But then the thrill changed to horror, and she heard herself calling for another lemonade.

"Wait, stop!" she cried. "I mean, *cut!* Rick—wha...what are you *doing?*"

Rick turned toward his director and said, in a matter-of-fact tone, "Well, I'm turning water into wine."

"But what's with all the arm-waving?" Lyn pleaded. "I'm sorry, Rick, but you make it look as if Jesus is some kind of wizard."

Rick looked at the other cast members, his brow furrowed. He raised his two upturned hands and asked, "But, well, *isn't* He?"

"Isn't He *what?*"

"Some kind of wizard."

It took another gulp of lemonade before Lyn could answer. "Heavens, no," she said. "Whatever gave you *that* idea?"

Rick scratched his head and explained, "I'm sorry, but I guess that just made sense to me. I don't yet know much about Jesus. You know, I just became a Christian."

"Yes, I know," Lyn said, "and I appreciate very much your willingness to serve right away. But what gave you the idea that Jesus was a...a wizard?"

"Well, the script has Him turning water into wine. And

later He raises a widow's son from the dead. After that He withers a tree just by speaking to it. I just assumed…"

Several younger members of the cast started giggling, and Jimmy Kerrings absent-mindedly took out a ketchup packet from his pocket and squeezed the contents into his mouth. "Gross!" said Nancy Hodgson, but no one else noticed.

"Rick, I see where you might get that, but believe me, Jesus was no wizard," Lyn said. "Let's try that scene again, but this time try to think of the Lord as less of a magician and more of the Son of God."

Rick nodded but continued to stand motionless. Either he was deep in thought or at a loss as to what to do next.

"Rick—is there a problem?"

"Well, to be honest," Rick said slowly, "I'm not exactly sure what the Son of God might act like. If He's not a wizard, do I play Him more like a king? In the script, He calls Himself the Lord of the Sabbath, and He says that God made Him the Judge of all. So do I play Him like a…a…*benevolent dictator?*" He seemed genuinely puzzled.

Lyn smiled nervously and took another sip of lemonade. "Well, that wouldn't be exactly right," she said. "Remember, the Lord also tells us that 'many who are first will be last, and the last first.' And He says, 'Do to others as you would have them do to you.' So He's not really a benevolent dictator."

A look of understanding began to burn in Rick's eyes

and he replied, "Oh, *I* see! He's really more like a philosopher! Is that right?"

Lyn tried to take another gulp of lemonade, but unhappily discovered she already had drained the cup. She looked around for Judy, the stage manager, but saw her nowhere. She realized she'd have to answer this one dry.

"No, Rick, that's not exactly right either," she said. Sighing deeply, she struggled for the appropriate words. "The Bible tells us that Jesus was utterly unique, the one-and-only Son of God, the perfect image of the Father. He did many miracles, but He wasn't a wizard. He was a king, but He didn't act like a dictator. He spoke wise words, but He wasn't a philosopher. Do you see?"

Silence reigned, and not even Jimmy Kerrings so much as reached for his bulging pocket. At last a small, frail woman spoke up from the front row. The voice belonged to Margaret Westerling, who at age eighty-two seemed perfect for the part of Anna, the elderly prophetess who celebrated the coming of God to Israel.[1] Margaret didn't speak often, but when she did, everyone listened.

"I think, young man," she said, "that you need more than our little script can give you. I recommend that you go home tonight and start reading the Gospels. Watch how Jesus treats people. Don't just look at what He says or the miracles He does, but observe how He interacts with His followers, with women, with children, with His opponents. Try to get a mental picture in your head of His personality. Can you do that?"

Rick nodded. "Sure, I can do that. That's a simple character study."

"Good," Margaret replied. "And, dear, may I give you one word of special advice?"

"Certainly," Rick said. Lyn nodded vigorously.

"Maybe you should start with John 13:14-15, where Jesus washes His disciples' feet. He reminds them that while He is their Teacher and Lord, He also came to serve. 'I have set you an example,' He says, 'that you should do as I have done for you.' I believe that one simple scene will give you a better idea of how to play the Savior than anything else. Plus," she said with a twinkle in her eye, "the exercise will give you a wonderful foundation for your new life as a Christian. I think you'll quickly begin to see what the apostle meant when he wrote, 'Whoever claims to live in him must walk as Jesus did.' That's 1 John 2:6, by the way."

"Thanks, Mrs…? " Rick replied.

"Westerling, but you can call me Anna," said Margaret with a laugh.

———

That night Rick Watson went home and began to read about Jesus. He followed "Anna's" advice and started with the story of how Jesus served His disciples by washing their feet, just before the Last Supper. He marveled at how this preeminent Teacher and Lord humbled Himself to meet the needs of His men—and how He explicitly told them to follow His example.

The night sped by as Rick watched Jesus interact with all kinds of people. He observed carefully as Jesus modeled for His followers how they ought to pray.[2] He rejoiced as he saw Jesus show compassion for the hurting and the weary.[3] He noted how his Lord depended upon the Holy Spirit[4] and marveled as he saw Jesus repeatedly refuse to use His power for selfish ends.[5]

By the time he finally went to bed, Rick began to see how he could portray Jesus in the Christmas play. As Lord, surely, but also as Servant; as Teacher, but also as Friend. Lyn Hafziger had been right to say that Jesus was one-of-a-kind! And yet, he knew, dear Mrs. Westerling also had been right in insisting that Jesus left us an example to follow. "Whoever claims to live in Him must walk as Jesus did," she had said, quoting the Bible, and now Rick had a much clearer idea of what that verse meant. In fact, the Jesus he read about in the Gospels reminded him a great deal of his father, a former elementary-school principal universally recognized as strong, kind, wise, and beloved. And he intended to show that kind of Jesus onstage.

Lyn Hafziger beamed. Somehow the chaos of the past few weeks had yielded a moving presentation on the life of Christ. If cast and crew could duplicate their successful dress rehearsal in their performances, she knew that Sonrise Community Church was in for a rare treat. Lyn took stock of the gains. A remarkable change had come over Rick Watson. Nancy Hodgson had learned to stop mugging. And even Jimmy Kerrings had finally given up his quest to soak the stage in ketchup.

"Lyn," said stage manager Judy Peterson, "it looks as if you did it! Congratulations!"

"Don't congratulate me," Lyn said. "Congratulate the cast. They're the ones who deserve it."

"Don't be so modest. You had an awful lot to do with this, Madame Director. So I say again: Congratulations!"

"Thank you," Lyn said. A thought occurred to her, and she added, "Oh, and Judy? Could I ask you to do one more thing?"

"I know, I know," Judy answered. "You'd like me to make sure we have enough lemonade for refreshments after the performance."

Lyn grinned. "Actually, no," she said. "I've had enough lemonade for one season. Can't we have some nice Christmas punch instead?"

S.H.

THIRTEEN

THERE'S NO PLACE LIKE HOME

And the angel said unto them, "Fear not: for, behold, I bring you good tidings of great joy, which shall be to all people. For unto you is born this day in the city of David a Saviour, which is Christ the Lord."

LUKE 2:10-11 (KJV)

*T*here's something special about being home for Christmas. It's amazing, almost supernatural.

At this time of year, people always ask you about home. If you're out on your own, they'll ask, "Are you going home for Christmas?" When you have grown children, they'll ask, "Are your children coming home for Christmas?" And when you're grandparents, they'll ask, "Are you going to be with your children this Christmas?"

Even after the holidays, people ask the same questions again and again: Did you see your family at Christmas? Did they come home? Did you go home?

The bottom line is we want to be home at Christmastime. Christmas is different from all other holidays!

At Easter, many people head south to the beach where it's warm. They do not especially want to be at home on Easter. For the Fourth of July, some go to the mountains where it's cool. On Labor Day, nearly everybody clears out— anywhere *but* home.

Christmas, however, is different. At Christmas, we just want to be at home. We want our families to be around us; home is the place to be. We might even say that Christmas is synonymous with *home.*

Yet a strange and almost ironic fact about the Nativity story is that not a single person in it was home that first Christmas!

Mary and Joseph lived in Nazareth but, on Christmas, they were in Bethlehem. They were not at home.

The shepherds were in the fields. They were not home with their families for Christmas. They were out tending the flock all night long.

The Magi were on the road to Israel. They were not at home in their comfortable palaces for Christmas. Instead, they were logging many hard miles on camelback as they made their way to Bethlehem.

No one was at home that first Christmas—and the one farthest from home was Jesus Christ. He left His home in heaven to make that long and amazing journey all the way to earth. The Logos, the eternal God, took on human form and became the Everlasting Father of everyone who will receive Him. Our Lord left home at Christmas so that we might be at home with Him forever.

What Is Home?

Most of us want to be home for Christmas, but very few of us have ever sat down to really ponder what *home* means. What does it mean to be home? How can we accurately define *home*?

For some, *home* means being with family. Others say, "Home is where our emotions are located, in the protected places of our heart." Still others define *home* as a specific geographical location or a particular house or apartment.

Think back to the Christmases of your own youth. What feelings do you associate with a sense of home? When I think about home, four traits or characteristics come to mind.

First, I think of home as a place of *security.* For many years, Christmas at my home meant gathering around the turkey and dressing. My mother would always make fruit-cake. We would have to tiptoe gently through the kitchen so the fruitcakes wouldn't fall (though I discovered they were much sweeter when they did). I also remember cutting down the Christmas tree with my father. I'll never forget the times we spent securing those trees and making them stand tall and straight. We all have our unique Christmas traditions. Some of us open gifts on Christmas Eve, while others insist on Christmas morning. We're all different—but our traditions and our memories give us that secure feeling that everything is okay.

Second, Christmas at home gave me a sense of *belonging.* At home we could take our shoes off. All of our little personal habits and quirks were in plain view of the family, but still we were loved and accepted. We knew where we stood in the family tree, what was expected of us, and what was expected of others. Belonging meant knowing who lived in the house on the corner or what streets to take for getting somewhere quickly. All the familiarities and remembrances made me feel that I belonged.

Third, home gave me a sense of *celebration.* I could always count on a Christmas full of fun with family and friends. Aunts and uncles often visited, embracing me and telling me how good I looked and how smart I was. They believed in me. On Christmas Day, my family celebrated by singing, reading the Christmas story, and unwrapping gifts. It was a joyful time when we felt secure and warm; it was easy to celebrate.

Fourth, home brought a sense of *optimism.* I remember some Christmases when I didn't get what I wanted, but I just *knew* I would get it next year. Another Christmas was always around the corner! Most of all, I remember my mom and dad saying to me, "Edwin, you can do anything in this world that you set your mind and heart on doing. You can do it."

The security, the celebration, the belonging, the optimism—they all explain why I liked to be home at Christmas. You're probably not so different from me. But before long, we grew up and got out on our own. The world beat us up, and then it beat us down. Relationships changed—and not always for the better. Optimism dimmed and soured into pessimism. Sometimes our best shot wasn't enough. Then the unthinkable happened. For some of us, parents split up. Financial adversity barged in. Health gave out. Loved ones died. And we realized that life wasn't turning out as we had planned.

And now Christmas has arrived once more, triggering all the old memories—some good, some bad. Yet for all of that, deep within us lives the desire for a renewed sense of security, belonging, celebration, and optimism.

This Christmas I want you to know that the Everlasting Father is speaking your name. Your name has been on His lips ten thousand times already, and it is on His lips today. He has thought about you today, and He knows how you feel. Your Savior knows you need a sense of family, a sense of home, and He says to you, "Fear not."

No Reason for Fear

Christmas first began on the hills of Judea as an angel announced the arrival of the Son of God. As he appeared to the shepherds, splitting the night sky with radiant light, he said, "Do not be afraid. I bring you good news of great joy that will be for all the people. Today in the town of David a Savior has been born to you; he is Christ the Lord" (Luke 2:10-11).

Did you know that the little phrase *Do not be afraid* appears more than 360 times in the Bible? Our Everlasting Father came at Christmas to give us the *security* most of us enjoyed when we were children. He is like a father who checks the doors and locks them tight before retiring for the evening. He closes all the windows to keep out the things of this world that lurk in the shadows. He tucks us into bed each night and assures us of His Presence for tomorrow. He looks in the closets and checks under the bed to reassure us that all is safe.

Along with security, Jesus also brings *belonging*. An angelic chorus announced the birth of our Savior, joyfully proclaiming that our Everlasting Father came to save us from our sins. Jesus paid the price of our sin, the cost of our adoption into the family of God. And now we belong fully to Him. He sought us out, He chose us, and He extended an invitation to enter His home and live with Him. God says to each of us, "I have made a way through My Son Jesus—once the Christmas Child and now your Everlasting Father—for you to belong to the family of God. Through His coming at Christmas and His leaving at Easter, repentant people like you can be adopted into My family. You will belong to Me in this life and throughout all eternity!" As members of the household of God, we find total forgiveness and complete acceptance, a sense of belonging that exceeds all of our best childhood memories.

Best of all, every one of these benefits is permanent. So how can we not *celebrate?* How can we not rejoice? How can we not throw parties and give gifts and bake cookies and string up pretty lights? Christmas is the "good news of great joy" that so thrilled the celebrating angels that they had to sing to the shepherds—or burst! The Everlasting Father came to give us eternal joy, a joy that cannot be taken away because God has given it. That's the celebration that comes with being at home with Jesus Christ.

And if we have all those things, how can we not be filled with *optimism?* Christmas is a time of joy, but it's also a time of hope. In our Everlasting Father, Jesus Christ, we have been given "a light for revelation to the Gentiles and for glory to your people Israel" (Luke 2:32). Jesus is a light "to shine on those living in darkness and in the shadow of death, to guide our feet into the path of peace" (Luke 1:79). Christmas looks forward to Easter, which in turn looks forward to the return of the King. The day is soon coming when Jesus Christ will return physically to this earth in great power and glory, bringing with Him His reward to bestow upon all who have looked forward to His appearing (2 Timothy 4:8). We ought to be the most optimistic people on earth!

The miracle of Christmas is that Jesus came to help you and me to feel at home whatever the circumstances of life. After all, we have the security, the belonging, the celebration, and the optimism that comes with being at home with Him.

Do you want to be home with the Everlasting Father this Christmas? Would you like to experience His eternal joy that no one can take away? Many of us know only Christmas at our earthly home, nothing more. It has become an annual event, observed in a place where there is no lasting peace, little security, and perhaps only a trickle of joy.

But the Everlasting Father says to you and to me, "You can be at home in Me this Christmas." We really can be at home in Him this season—no matter where we are or what we have been doing.

LIGHT UP YOUR LIFE

Do you know what the Everlasting Father can do for you this Christmas if you let Him? He'll light up your life! John talks about this in his gospel, where he tells us that Jesus came as "light" (John 1:4). And Jesus Himself said, "I am the light of the world" (John 8:12).

What does light do? Light accomplishes at least three things:

- It illuminates.
- It warms.
- It causes growth.

As Christmas Day approaches, what darkness, if any, is in your life? What oppression is in your world? Do you feel depressed, bored, or as though everything looks dark and negative? This Christmas let the Everlasting Father illuminate your world. He'll light up your life.

Do you feel cold today? Cynical? Maybe the world has beaten you up, or you feel as though you've somehow missed your calling. You wonder if you're on track. If your days feel cold and stale, invite Jesus to give you warmth and vitality. He will warm your heart, your motives, and your mind. You will feel a warmth that you've never known. The Everlasting Father is in the business of radiating a warm, healing light.

Or do you feel as though you're not growing? Maybe life has come to a stop, and you've seen no progress for a long time. Does your life seem to have any movement, or is today like tomorrow, which was just like the day before? Are you just waiting for something to happen? This Christmas, let Jesus be a stimulus for growth.

As natural light causes growth, so does the Light of the World. He illuminates us, warms us, and causes us to grow. So why not spend this Christmas embracing the Everlasting Father? Let Him shine within your life.

Believe me, you really can go home again—even if you've never been there before.

E.Y.

FOURTEEN

THE COMPOSITION

Then they brought him a demon-possessed man who was blind and mute, and Jesus healed him, so that he could both talk and see. All the people were astonished and said, "Could this be the Son of David?"

MATTHEW 12:22-23

ear Maestro:
I beg you to forgive me for writing, uninvited, to such an accomplished composer and lyricist as yourself, but I am in dire straits. For this year's celebration of Soncome, I have been asked by my choral section here at the university to develop new lyrics to an ancient tune of my choosing. The song is supposed to be bright and happy and energetic, reminding us all that the King has *always* reigned in majesty, even in ancient days. I am not sure why they chose me for this task—I don't know ancient hymnody all that well and

have never written great lyrics—but my professor made it abundantly clear that the job is mine and no one else's. I am allowed to seek help, however, and that is why I am reaching out to you. As a distinguished alumnus of this school, is there any way you could provide me with some guidance? Anything? *Please?*

Faithfully yours,
Ludwig von Handel

My dear Ludwig:
I would be delighted to provide whatever assistance may be appropriate. As to possible recommendations for an "ancient tune," as you put it, I suggest you spend some time in the "Christmas" section of the school archives. You might narrow your search to the period between 600 and 800 B.C.R.* The university's recordings from that era have hardly degraded at all, and I believe you will find something suitable for your needs.

As to lyrics, I often have found it useful to take inspiration both from current events and from the unchanging Word of God. You say your college would like lyrics that proclaim that "the King has *always* reigned in majesty, even in ancient days," so might I suggest a two-pronged attack?

---

* Before Christ Returned.

First, ask yourself a question: What best suggests majesty to you? To my mind, the King most expresses His majesty in the way He constantly amazes, continually astonishes, perpetually surprises. For centuries now He has reigned physically among us from His throne in Jerusalem, yet every day He offers unexpected and delightful revelations of His glory. Why don't you spend some time in His Word, looking especially for those occasions when He amazed and astonished those who witnessed His ministry so long ago? As He amazes us today, so He did in ancient times, even when He veiled His full glory from human eyes.

Second, you might consider how to use current events to shape your musical creation. Permit me to give you an example. As you know, composers the world over turn their focus every year to one selected aspect of the King's character. This year we have been concentrating on the Son of David as our "Everlasting Father," as the prophet Isaiah saw Him. So you might ask yourself, "How does my Everlasting Father amaze me?"

Ludwig, I pray that this assignment benefits not only you, but all those privileged to study at my old school. Please keep me informed of your progress.

> *In the service of the King,*
> *Julius DeVento*

Dear Maestro DeVento:

Thank you *so much* for your tremendous guidance! I feel I have made great progress since I first contacted you. I did as you suggested and visited the archives, and I have chosen a little-known piece called "The Twelve Days of Christmas." I liked the merry tune, although I did not much understand the lyrics. But since I am to write new lines anyway, I doubt that matters.

I also took your advice and scoured the Holy Scriptures for amazing events in our Lord's first earthly ministry. What a joy that has been! Again, I hope you will not mind my boldness—after all, you did encourage me to keep you updated on my progress—but I would like to reproduce for you the first few lyrics I have written.

But first, perhaps, I should explain that each of my lines found its inspiration from the following gospel stories: Matthew 21:19, where our Lord, through a mere word, withers a fruitless fig tree; Matthew 8:28-32, where the Savior frees two men from demonic possession; Matthew 12:40, where the Messiah prophesies that He would spend three days and nights in the grave before rising from the dead; Matthew 17:27, where the King directs Peter to pay a tax by finding a coin in the mouth of a fish; and Matthew 14:17, where our Lord feeds a hungry multitude with just five loaves of bread and two fish.

Astonishing stories, all! I am not quite halfway through my song—I am trying to mimic some of the ancient structure, as you will see—but I will show you what I have written so far:

> On the first day of Soncome, my Father gave to me,
>   a cursed and a withered fig tree.
> On the second day of Soncome, my Father gave to me,
>   two exorcisms and a cursed and a withered fig tree.
> On the third day of Soncome, my Father gave to me,
>   three days in Hades, two exorcisms, and a cursed and
>   a withered fig tree.
> On the fourth day of Soncome, my Father gave to me,
>   a four-drachma coin, three days in Hades, two
>   exorcisms, and a cursed and a withered fig tree.
> On the fifth day of Soncome, my Father gave to me, five
>   bread loaves! A four-drachma coin, three days in
>   Hades, two exorcisms, and a cursed and a withered
>   fig tree.

Sir, I am stuck there, for now. Do you like it? What do you think, honestly? Am I onto something here? I hope so.

> *Thankful for your collaboration,*
> *Ludwig von Handel*

Dear Ludwig:

While I feel profoundly blessed that you have found my advice helpful, may I encourage you to rethink your creative direction? I do not at all mean to be critical, but I must point out that the song as you have it falls somewhat…short of its lofty purpose. A song to be performed in celebration of the glorious return of Christ must be emotionally fulfilling as well as faithful to the Holy Scriptures. While I am quite sure that many might consider your current lyrics astonishing, I feel obliged to point out that most lyricists, myself included, often find it necessary to rewrite. I believe that would be best in this case.

> *Hoping for the best,*
> *Julius DeVento*

P.S. Since I have no desire to steal *any* of the credit due you for your hard work, perhaps it would be best if you would refrain from mentioning to anyone at the university that I have given you counsel (not collaboration) in your efforts.

Dear Maestro DeVento:

It is as I feared; my meager talents are not up to the task. I do not know why they insisted that I take on this job since it is clearly beyond me. Thank you for your valuable time and assistance. I assure you that I will not tell anyone of your involvement. I completely realize that the blame is my own, alone. You have been gracious in responding to me at all, and I shall waste no more of your time.

Still grateful for your kindness,
Ludwig von Handel

My dearest Ludwig:

I am deeply ashamed of myself. You came to me for help, and I was willing to give it…so long as it reflected well upon me. Yet as soon as the lyrics got a little bumpy, so to speak, I tried (as you rightly saw) to disassociate myself from the proceedings. That is neither helpful nor godly, and I beg your forgiveness. If you are willing, I propose that together we shall see this thing through—and you may tell anyone you care to about our *collaboration*. So again, I pledge to give whatever assistance I may.

And yet, I must remind you, the job is largely yours. The university has made that clear. I will give what advice seems useful, but you must craft the lyrics.

First, I think your choice of song (in ancient times they called it a carol) will work just fine. Did you know that the original line about a "partridge in a pear tree" really referred to Jesus Christ? So you have chosen most appropriately.

Second, while I see that you have done some good research into the amazing deeds of our Lord during His first Advent, may I suggest that you haven't gone back in time quite far enough? Remember, He is the *Everlasting* Father. Long before that first Christmas, He counted us His dear children and did for us what His fatherly nature loved to do—namely, He astonished us with surprising deeds that left us breathless and marveling.

"O LORD, you are my God," wrote Isaiah. "I will exalt you and praise your name, for in perfect faithfulness you have done *marvelous* things, things planned long ago" (Isaiah 25:1).

Do you recall what Moses told his people as they prepared to enter the Promised Land, a dangerous country full of powerful enemies? "Then I said to you, 'Do not be terrified; do not be afraid of them. The LORD your God, who is going before you, will fight for you, as he did for you in Egypt, before your very eyes, and in the desert. There you saw how the LORD your God carried you, *as a father carries his son,* all the way you went until you reached this place'" (Deuteronomy 1:29-31).

Who do you think did the carrying? Was it not our Everlasting Father, Jesus Christ? Or who do you suppose Joshua spoke of when he told the Israelites, "Consecrate yourselves, for tomorrow the LORD will do *amazing* things among you"

(Joshua 3:5). Was it not the King who now reigns over all the world from His throne in Jerusalem?

Did not our Everlasting Father often say, during His first Advent, "The stone the builders rejected has become the capstone; the LORD has done this, and it is *marvelous* in our eyes" (Psalm 118:22-23)?

You have studied well, Ludwig, the marvelous things our Everlasting Father did on earth during His time with His apostles, but have you considered what the prophets said of Him regarding our own time? The prophet Zechariah writes, "This is what the LORD Almighty says: 'Once again men and women of ripe old age will sit in the streets of Jerusalem, each with cane in hand because of his age. The city streets will be filled with boys and girls playing there.' This is what the LORD Almighty says: 'It may seem *marvelous* to the remnant of this people at that time, but will it seem *marvelous* to me?' declares the LORD Almighty" (Zechariah 8:4-6).

Don't you see, Ludwig? If your goal is to sing of how the Everlasting Father has always reigned in majesty, even in ancient days, then you should use the opportunity to remind your audience that the King cannot and never could do *other* than amaze. He amazed us in Moses' day; He amazed us in Joshua's day; He amazed us in the apostles' day; and He amazes us today. In fact, to be the Everlasting Father *is* to astonish!

Now, Ludwig, get *that* into your lyrics, and then you'll have something worth singing about!

> *Delighted to serve with you,*
> *Julius DeVento*

Dear Maestro DeVento:

Sir, you don't know how much your last letter encouraged me. I was ready to drop out of this school and look for somewhere to disappear, but then I received and devoured your gracious words. I still do not know why the school insists that *I* write this song, but I will give it my best effort. Of that you may be sure!

I love your idea about how the Lord amazes us from start to finish. I've been thinking about the passages you mentioned, and I wonder whether the following first line might work?

> *On the first day of Soncome, my Father gave to me,*
> *a wise plan to set my heart free.*

Do you think, Maestro, that this might be a better start? It takes us all the way back to the beginning and expresses so well the joy of my own heart. Do you think this "works"?

> *Encouraged to begin again,*
> *Ludwig von Handel*

To My beloved Ludwig and My dear friend Julius:

How you both fill Me with joy! Your efforts have not gone unnoticed (or unappreciated!), and I want you to know that both of you may expect something special from Jerusalem this Christmas. I have long delighted in saying that if anyone gives even a cup of cold water to a little one because he is My disciple, he will certainly not lose his reward.[1]

Ludwig, it was I who requested that you be allowed to choose the tune and write the lyrics for this year's Soncome celebration. You have done well, although you have often doubted it! I want you to know that I will personally be present when your choral group presents your work. I wouldn't miss it for the world.

I am equally pleased with you, Julius, for taking seriously your role as mentor. It was I who chose you to encourage My son Ludwig, though you did not know it. Your "cup of cold water" reached him at just the right time. How did I know? A Father knows these things.

Refreshed at your hands,
Your devoted Everlasting Father

S.H.

NOTES

Introduction

1. Adapted from *The Nicene and Post-Nicene Fathers, First Series, Volume 10, Saint Chrysostom: Homilies on the Gospel of Saint Matthew* (Peabody, Mass.: Hendrickson, 1994), 47.

Chapter 1

1. For those who can't come up with the right answers, here they are:
   What do elves learn in school? *The elf-abet.*
   What do snowmen eat for breakfast? *Frosted flakes.*
   What kind of candle burns longer, a red one or a green one? *Neither; candles always burn shorter.*
   Why was Santa's little helper depressed? *He had low elf-esteem.*

2. D. E. Hiebert, in *The Zondervan Pictorial Encyclopedia of the Bible,* vol. 5, ed. Merrill C. Tenney (Grand Rapids, Mich.: Zondervan, 1976), 172.

3. First stanza from "Of the Father's Love Begotten," from thirteenth-century plainsong.

Chapter 2

1. Frederick Buechner, *The Hungering Dark* (New York: HarperCollins, 1969), 14.

Chapter 3

1. Matthew 8:14-17.
2. Matthew 8:23-27; 14:22-33.
3. Luke 22:31-62; John 18:10-11.
4. Acts 12:6-11.
5. John 21:15-19.

Chapter 6

1. Luke 8:2.
2. Luke 8:3.
3. Matthew 11:28-29.
4. Matthew 12:43.
5. Matthew 16:27.
6. Luke 12:49,51-53.
7. Matthew 12:40.
8. Matthew 20:18-19.
9. Matthew 28:5-6.

Chapter 12

1. Luke 2:36-38.
2. Matthew 6:9-13.

3. Matthew 15:32.
4. Luke 4:14.
5. Matthew 4:1-11; 26:53.

Chapter 14
1. Matthew 10:42.